PENGUIN

LIFE AT GRASMERE

Dorothy
and
William
Wordsworth

English 🐧 *Journeys*

PENGUIN BOOKS

Published by the Penguin Group
Penguin Books Ltd, 80 Strand, London WC2R ORL, England
Penguin Group (USA) Inc., 375 Hudson Street, New York, New York 10014, USA
Penguin Group (Canada), 90 Eglinton Avenue East, Suite 700, Toronto, Ontario, Canada M4P 2Y3
(a division of Pearson Penguin Canada Inc.)
Penguin Ireland, 25 St Stephen's Green, Dublin 2, Ireland
(a division of Penguin Books Ltd)
Penguin Group (Australia), 250 Camberwell Road, Camberwell, Victoria 3124, Australia
(a division of Pearson Australia Group Pty Ltd)
Penguin Books India Pvt Ltd, 11 Community Centre, Panchsheel Park, New Delhi – 110 017, India
Penguin Group (NZ), 67 Apollo Drive, Rosedale, North Shore 0632, New Zealand
(a division of Pearson New Zealand Ltd)
Penguin Books (South Africa) (Pty) Ltd, 24 Sturdee Avenue, Rosebank, Johannesburg 2196, South Africa

Penguin Books Ltd, Registered Offices: 80 Strand, London WC2R ORL, England

www.penguin.com

This selection from *Home at Grasmere* first published 1986
Published in Penguin Books 2009

3

All rights reserved

Set by Rowland Phototypesetting Ltd, Bury St Edmunds, Suffolk
Printed in England by Clays Ltd, St Ives plc

978-0-141-19100-3

www.greenpenguin.co.uk

Penguin Books is committed to a sustainable future
for our business, our readers and our planet.
The book in your hands is made from paper
certified by the Forest Stewardship Council.

Soon after the Wordsworths had settled at Grasmere, William began a long philosophical poem called 'The Recluse'. He never finished it; but the first part, printed below, serves to set the scene at Grasmere.

The Recluse

PART FIRST

Book First – Home at Grasmere

Once to the verge of yon steep barrier came
A roving school-boy; what the adventurer's age
Hath now escaped his memory – but the hour,
One of a golden summer holiday
He well remembers, though the year be gone –
Alone and devious from afar he came;
And, with a sudden influx overpowered
At sight of this seclusion, he forgot
His haste, for hasty had his footsteps been
As boyish his pursuits; and sighing said,
'What happy fortune were it here to live!
And, if a thought of dying, if a thought
Of mortal separation, could intrude
With paradise before him, here to die!'

No Prophet was he, had not even a hope,
Scarcely a wish, but one bright pleasing thought,
A fancy in the heart of what might be
The lot of others, never could be his.
    The station whence he looked was soft and green,
Not giddy yet aerial, with a depth
Of vale below, a height of hills above.
For rest of body perfect was the spot,
All that luxurious nature could desire;
But stirring to the spirit; who could gaze
And not feel motions there? He thought of clouds
That sail on winds: of breezes that delight
To play on water, or in endless chase
Pursue each other through the yielding plain
Of grass or corn, over and through and through,
In billow after billow, evermore
Disporting – nor unmindful was the boy
Of sunbeams, shadows, butterflies and birds;
Of fluttering sylphs and softly-gliding Fays,
Genii, and winged angels that are Lords
Without restraint of all which they behold.
The illusion strengthening as he gazed, he felt
That such unfettered liberty was his,
Such power and joy; but only for this end,
To flit from field to rock, from rock to field,
From shore to island, and from isle to shore,
From open ground to covert, from a bed
Of meadow-flowers into a tuft of wood;
From high to low, from low to high, yet still
Within the bound of this huge concave; here
Must be his home, this valley be his world.

Since that day forth the Place to him – *to me*
(For I who live to register the truth
Was the same young and happy Being) became
As beautiful to thought, as it had been
When present, to the bodily sense; a haunt
Of pure affections, shedding upon joy
A brighter joy; and through such damp and gloom
Of the gay mind, as oftimes splenetic youth
Makes for sorrow, darting beams of light
That no self-cherished sadness could withstand;
And now 'tis mine, perchance for life, dear Vale
Beloved Grasmere (let the wandering streams
Take up, the cloud-capt hills repeat, the Name)
One of thy lowly Dwellings is my Home.

And was the cost so great? and could it seem
An act of courage, and the thing itself
A conquest? who must bear the blame? Sage man
Thy prudence, thy experience, thy desires,
Thy apprehensions – blush thou for them all.

Yes the realities of life so cold,
So cowardly, so ready to betray,
So stinted in the measure of their grace
As we pronounce them, doing them much wrong,
Have been to me more bountiful than hope,
Less timid than desire – but that is past.

On Nature's invitation do I come,
By Reason sanctioned. Can the choice mislead,
That made the calmest fairest spot of earth
With all its unappropriated good
My own; and not mine only, for with me
Entrenched, say rather peacefully embowered,

Under yon orchard, in yon humble cot,
A younger Orphan of a home extinct,
The only Daughter of my Parents dwells.
   Ay, think on that, my heart, and cease to stir,
Pause upon that and let the breathing frame
No longer breathe, but all be satisfied.
– Oh, if such silence be not thanks to God
For what hath been bestowed, then where, where then
Shall gratitude find rest? Mine eyes did ne'er
Fix on a lovely object, nor my mind
Take pleasure in the midst of happy thoughts,
But either She whom now I have, who now
Divides with me this loved abode, was there,
Or not far off. Where'er my footsteps turned,
Her voice was like a hidden Bird that sang.
The thought of her was like a flash of light,
Or an unseen companionship, a breath
Of fragrance independent of the Wind.
In all my goings, in the new and old
Of all my meditations, and in this
Favourite of all, in this the most of all.
– What being, therefore, since the birth of Man
Had ever more abundant cause to speak
Thanks, and if favours of the Heavenly Muse
Make him more thankful, then to call on Verse
To aid him and in song resound his joy?
The boon is absolute; surpassing grace
To me hath been vouchsafed; among the bowers
Of blissful Eden this was neither given
Nor could be given, possession of the good
Which had been sighed for, ancient thought fulfilled,

And dear Imagination realised,
Up to their highest measure, yea and more.
    Embrace me then, ye Hills, and close me in;
Now in the clear and open day I feel
Your guardianship; I take it to my heart;
'Tis like the solemn shelter of the night.
But I would call thee beautiful, for mild,
And soft, and gay, and beautiful thou art
Dear Valley, having in thy face a smile
Though peaceful, full of gladness. Thou art pleased,
Pleased with thy crags and woody steeps, thy Lake,
Its one green island and its winding shores;
The multitude of little rocky hills,
Thy Church and cottages of mountain stone
Clustered like stars some few, but single most,
And lurking dimly in their shy retreats,
Or glancing at each other cheerful looks
Like separated stars with clouds between.
What want we? have we not perpetual streams,
Warm woods, and sunny hills, and fresh green fields,
And mountains not less green, and flocks and herds,
And thickets full of songsters, and the voice
Of lordly birds, an unexpected sound
Heard now and then from morn to latest eve,
Admonishing the man who walks below
Of solitude and silence in the sky?
These have we, and a thousand nooks of earth
Have also these, but nowhere else is found,
Nowhere (or it is fancy?) can be found
The one sensation that is here; 'tis here,
Here as it found its way into my heart

In childhood, here as it abides by day,
By night, here only; or in chosen minds
That take it with them hence, where'er they go.
– 'Tis, but I cannot name it, 'tis the sense
Of majesty, and beauty, and repose,
A blended holiness of earth and sky,
Something that makes this individual spot,
This small abiding-place of many men,
A termination, and a last retreat,
A centre, come from wheresoe'er you will,
A whole without dependence or defect,
Made for itself, and happy in itself,
Perfect contentment, Unity entire.

    Bleak season was it, turbulent and bleak,
When hitherward we journeyed side by side
Through burst of sunshine and through flying showers;
Paced the long vales – how long they were – and yet
How fast that length of way was left behind,
Wensley's rich Vale, and Sedbergh's naked heights.
The frosty wind, as if to make amends
For its keen breath, was aiding to our steps,
And drove us onward like two ships at sea,
Or like two birds, companions in mid-air,
Parted and reunited by the blast.

    Stern was the face of nature; we rejoiced
In that stern countenance, for our souls thence drew
A feeling of their strength. The naked trees,
The icy brook, as on we passed, appeared
To question us. 'Whence come ye, to what end?'
They seemed to say, 'What would ye,' said the shower,
'Wild Wanderers, whither through my dark domain?'

The sunbeam said, 'Be happy.' When this vale
We entered, bright and solemn was the sky
That faced us with a passionate welcoming,
And led us to our threshold. Daylight failed
Insensibly, and round us gently fell
Composing darkness, with a quiet load
Of full contentment, in a little shed
Disturbed, uneasy in itself as seemed,
And wondering at its new inhabitants.
It loves us now, this Vale so beautiful
Begins to love us! by a sullen storm,
Two months unwearied of severest storm,
It put the temper of our minds to proof,
And found us faithful through the gloom, and heard
The poet mutter his prelusive songs
With cheerful heart, an unknown voice of joy
Among the silence of the woods and hills;
Silent to any gladsomeness of sound
With all their shepherds.

I

'God be thanked, I want not
society by a moonlight lake.'

May 14th, 1800 [*Wednesday*]. Wm. and John set off into
Yorkshire after dinner at ½ past 2 o'clock, cold pork in
their pockets. I left them at the turning of the Lowwood
bay under the trees. My heart was so full that I could
hardly speak to W. when I gave him a farewell kiss. I
sate a long time upon a stone at the margin of the lake,
and after a flood of tears my heart was easier. The lake
looked to me, I knew not why, dull and melancholy, and
the weltering on the shores seemed a heavy sound. I
walked as long as I could amongst the stones of the
shore. The wood rich in flowers; a beautiful yellow,
palish yellow, flower, that looked thick, round, and
double, and smelt very sweet – I supposed it was a
ranunculus. Crowfoot, the grassy-leaved rabbit-toothed
white flower, strawberries, geranium, scentless violets,
anemones two kinds, orchise, primroses. The heckberry
very beautiful, the crab coming out as a low shrub. Met
a blind man, driving a very large beautiful Bull, and
a cow – he walked with two sticks. Came home by
Clappersgate. The valley very green; many sweet views
up to Rydale head, when I could juggle away the fine

9

houses; but they disturbed me, even more than when I have been happier; one beautiful view of the Bridge, without Sir Michael's. Sate down very often, though it was cold. I resolved to write a journal of the time till W. and J. return, and I set about keeping my resolve, because I will not quarrel with myself, and because I shall give Wm. pleasure by it when he comes home again. At Rydale, a woman of the village, stout and well dressed, begged a half-penny; she had never she said done it before, but these hard times! Arrived at home with a bad headach, set some slips of privett, the evening cold, had a fire, my face now flame-coloured. It is nine o'clock. I shall soon go to bed. A young woman begged at the door – she had come from Manchester on Sunday morn. with two shillings and a slip of paper which she supposed a Bank note – it was a cheat. She had buried her husband and three children within a year and a half – all in one grave – burying very dear – paupers all put in one place – 20 shillings paid for as much ground as will bury a man – a stone to be put over it or the right will be lost – 11/6 each time the ground is opened . . . Oh! that I had a letter from William!

May 15th, Thursday. A coldish dull morning – hoed the first row of peas, weeded etc. etc., sat hard to mending till evening. The rain which had threatened all day came on just when I was going to walk.

[*May 16th,*] *Friday morning.* Warm and mild, after a fine night of rain. Transplanted radishes after breakfast, walked to Mr Gell's with the books, gathered mosses and plants. The woods extremely beautiful with all autumnal variety and softness. I carried a basket for mosses, and gathered some wild plants. Oh! that we had a book of botany. All flowers now are gay and deliciously sweet. The primroses still pre-eminent among the later flowers of the spring. Foxgloves very tall, with their heads budding. I went forward round the lake at the foot of Loughrigg Fell. I was much amused with the business of a pair of stonechats; their restless voices as they skimmed along the water following each other, their shadows under them, and their returning back to the stones on the shore, chirping with the same unwearied voice. Could not cross the water, so I went round by the stepping-stones. The morning clear but cloudy, that is the hills were not overhung by mists. After dinner Aggy weeded onions and carrots. I helped for a little – wrote to Mary Hutchinson – washed my head – worked. After tea went to Ambleside – a pleasant cool but not cold evening. Rydale was very beautiful, with spear-shaped streaks of polished steel. No letters! – only one newspaper. I returned to Clappersgate. Grasmere was very solemn in the last glimpse of twilight; it calls home the heart to quietness. I had been very melancholy in my walk back. I had many of my saddest thoughts, and I could not keep the tears within me. But when I came to Grasmere I felt that it did me good. I finished my letter to M. H. Ate hasty pudding and went to bed. As I was going out in the morning I met a half crazy old man. He shewed me a pincushion and begged a pin, afterwards a half-penny. He began in a kind of indistinct voice in this manner: 'Matthew Jobson's lost a cow. Tom Nichol has two good horses strayed. Jim Jones's cow's brokken her horn, etc. etc.' He went into Aggy's and persuaded her to give him some whey, and let him boil some porridge. She declares he ate two quarts.

[*May 17th,*] *Saturday*. Incessant rain from morning till night. T. Ashburner brought us coals. Worked hard, and read *Midsummer Night's Dream*, [and] Ballads – sauntered a little in the garden. The Skobby [chaffinch] sate quietly in its nest, rocked by the wind, and beaten by the rain.

[*May*] *18th, Sunday*. Went to church, slight showers, a cold air. The mountains from this window look much greener, and I think the valley is more green than ever. The corn begins to shew itself. The ashes are still bare, went part of the way home with Miss Simpson. A little girl from Coniston came to beg. She had lain out all night – her step-mother had turned her out of doors. Her father could not stay at home 'she flights so'. Walked to Ambleside in the evening round the lake, the prospect exceedingly beautiful from Loughrigg Fell. It was so green that no eye could be weary of reposing upon it. The most beautiful situation for a house in the field next to Mr Benson's. It threatened rain all the evening but was mild and pleasant. I was overtaken by 2 Cumberland people on the other side of Rydale who complimented me upon my walking. They were going to sell cloth, and odd things which they make themselves, in Hawkshead and the neighbourhood. The post was not arrived, so I walked thro' the town, past Mrs Taylor's, and met him. Letters from Coleridge and Cottle. John

Fisher overtook me on the other side of Rydale. He talked much about the alteration in the times, and observed that in a short time there would be only two ranks of people, the very rich and the very poor, 'for those who have small estates', says he, 'are forced to sell, and all the land goes into one hand'. Did not reach home till 10 o'clock.

[*May 19th,*] *Monday.* Sauntered a good deal in the garden, bound carpets, mended old clothes. Read *Timon of Athens*. Dried linen. Molly weeded the turnips, John stuck the peas. We had not much sunshine or wind, but no rain till about 7 o'clock, when we had a slight shower just after I had set out upon my walk. I did not return but walked up into the Black Quarter. I sauntered a long time among the rocks above the church. The most delightful situation possible for a cottage, commanding two distinct views of the vale and of the lake, is among those rocks. I strolled on, gathered mosses etc. The quietness and still seclusion of the valley affected me even to producing the deepest melancholy. I forced myself from it. The wind rose before I went to bed. No rain – Dodwell and Wilkinson called in my absence.

[*May 20th,*] *Tuesday Morning.* A fine mild rain. After breakfast the sky cleared and before the clouds passed from the hills I went to Ambleside. It was a sweet morning. Everything green and overflowing with life, and the streams making a perpetual song, with the thrushes and all little birds, not forgetting the stone-chats. The post was not come in. I walked as far as Windermere, and met him there. No letters! no papers. Came home by Clappersgate. I was sadly tired, ate a hasty dinner and had a bad headach – went to bed and slept at least 2 hours. Rain came on in the evening – Molly washing.

May 26th, Monday. A very fine morning, worked in the garden till after 10 when old Mr Simpson came and talked to me till after 12. Molly weeding – wrote letters to J. H., Coleridge, C. Ll., and W. I walked towards Rydale, and turned aside at my favorite field. The air and the lake were still – one cottage light in the vale, and so much of day left that I could distinguish objects, the woods, trees and houses. Two or three different kinds of birds sang at intervals on the opposite shore. I sate till I could hardly drag myself away. I grew so sad. 'When pleasant thoughts', etc . . .

Lines Written in Early Spring

WRITTEN AT ALFOXDEN IN 1798

I heard a thousand blended notes,
While in a grove I sate reclined,
In that sweet mood when pleasant thoughts
Bring sad thoughts to the mind.

To her fair works did Nature link
The human soul that through me ran;
And much it grieved my heart to think
What man has made of man.

Through primrose tufts, in that green bower,
The periwinkle trailed its wreaths;
And 'tis my faith that every flower
Enjoys the air it breathes.

The birds around me hopped and played,
Their thoughts I cannot measure:–
But the least motion which they made
It seemed a thrill of pleasure.

The budding twigs spread out their fan,
To catch the breezy air;
And I must think, do all I can,
That there was pleasure there.

If this belief from heaven be sent,
If such be Nature's holy plan,
Have I not reason to lament
What man has made of man?

[*May*] 27th, *Tuesday*. I walked to Ambleside with letters –
met the post before I reached Mr Partridge's, one paper,
only a letter for Coleridge. I expected a letter from Wm.
It was a sweet morning, the ashes in the valley nearly in
full leaf, but still to be distinguished, quite bare on the
higher ground. I was warm in returning, and becoming
cold with sitting in the house I had a bad headach – went
to bed after dinner, and lay till after 5. Not well after tea.
I worked in the garden, but did not walk further. A
delightful evening before the sun set, but afterwards it
grew colder – mended stockings etc.

*

[*May 28th,*] *Wednesday*. In the morning walked up to the rocks above Jenny Dockeray's, sate a long time upon the grass, the prospect divinely beautiful. If I had three hundred pounds, and could afford to have a bad interest for my money, I would buy that estate, and we would build a cottage there to end our days in. I went into her garden and got white and yellow lilies, periwinkle, etc., which I planted. Sate under the trees with my work. No fire in the morning. Worked till between 7 and 8, and then watered the garden, and was about to go up to Mr Simpson's, when Miss S. and her visitors passed the door. I went home with them, a beautiful evening, the crescent moon hanging above Helm Crag.

June 1st, Sunday. Rain in the night – a sweet mild morning. Read Ballads; went to church. Singers from Wytheburn, went part of the way home with Miss Simpson. Walked upon the hill above the house till dinner time – went again to church – Christening and singing which kept us very late. The pewside came down with me. Walked with Mr Simpson nearly home. After tea, went to Ambleside, round the lakes – a very fine warm evening. I lay upon the steep of Loughrigg, my heart dissolved in what I saw, when I was not startled but re-called from my reverie by a noise as of a child paddling without shoes. I looked up and saw a lamb close to me. It approached nearer and nearer, as if to examine me, and stood a long time. I did not move. At last it ran past me, and went bleating along the pathway, seeming to be seeking its mother. I saw a hare on the high road. The post was not come in; waited in the road till John's apprentice came with a letter from Coleridge and 3 papers. The moon shone upon the water – reached home at 10 o'clock, went to bed immediately. Molly brought daisies etc. which we planted.

[*June 2nd,*] *Monday*. A cold dry windy morning. I worked in the garden, and planted flowers, etc. Sate under the trees after dinner till tea time. John Fisher stuck the peas, Molly weeded and washed. I went to Ambleside after tea, crossed the stepping-stone at the foot of Grasmere, and pursued my way on the other side of Rydale and by Clappersgate. I sate a long time to watch the hurrying waves, and to hear the regularly irregular sound of the dashing waters. The waves round about the little Island seemed like a dance of spirits that rose out of the water, round its small circumference of shore. Inquired about lodgings for Coleridge, and was accompanied by Mrs Nicholson as far as Rydale. This was very kind, but God be thanked, I want no society by a moonlight lake. It was near 11 when I reached home. I wrote to Coleridge, and went late to bed.

[*June 3rd,*] *Tuesday*. I sent off my letter by the Butcher. A boisterous drying day. I worked in the garden before dinner. Read *R[ichar]d Second* – was not well after dinner and lay down. Mrs Simpson's grandson brought me some gooseberries. I got up and walked with him part of the way home, afterwards went down rambling by the lake side – got Lockety Goldings, strawberries etc., and planted. Afted tea the wind fell. I walked towards Mr Simpson's, gave the newspapers to the Girl, reached home at 10. No letter, no William – a letter from R[ichar]d to John.

[*June 4th,*] *Wednesday.* A very fine day. I sate out of doors most of the day, wrote to Mr Jackson. Ambleside Fair. I walked to the lake-side in the morning, took up plants, and sate upon a stone reading Ballads. In the evening I was watering plants when Mr and Miss Simpson called. I accompanied them home, and we went to the waterfall at the head of the valley. It was very interesting in the Twilight. I brought home lemon thyme, and several other plants, and planted them by moonlight. I lingered out of doors in the hope of hearing my Brother's tread.

[*June 5th,*] *Tuesday.* I sate out of doors great part of the day and worked in the garden – had a letter from Mr Jackson, and wrote an answer to Coleridge. The little birds busy making love, and pecking the blossoms and bits of moss off the trees; they flutter about and about, and thrid the trees as I lie under them. Molly went out to tea, I would not go far from home, expecting my Brothers. I rambled on the hill above the house, gathered wild thyme, and took up roots of wild columbine. Just as I was returning with my load, Mr and Miss Simpson called. We went again upon the hill, got more plants, set them, and then went to the Blind Man's for London Pride for Miss Simpson. I went up with them as far as the Blacksmith's, a fine lovely moonlight night.

[*June 6th,*] *Friday.* Sate out of doors reading the whole afternoon, but in the morning I wrote to my aunt Cookson. In the evening I went to Ambleside with Coleridge's letter – it was a lovely night as the day had been. I went by Loughrigg and Clappersgate and just met the post at the turnpike; he told me there were two letters but none for me, so I was in no hurry and went round again by Clappersgate, crossed the stepping-stones and entered Ambleside at Matthew Harrison's. A letter from Jack Hutchinson, and one from Montagu, enclosing a 3£ note. No William! I slackened my pace as I came near home, fearing to hear that he was not come. I listened till after one o'clock to every barking dog, cock-fighting, and other sports: it was Mr Borwick's opening. Foxgloves just coming into blossom.

[*June 7th,*] *Saturday*. A very warm cloudy morning, threatening to rain. I walked up to Mr Simpson's to gather gooseberries – it was a very fine afternoon. Little Tommy came down with me, ate gooseberry pudding and drank tea with me. We went up the hill, to gather sods and plants, and went down to the lake side, and took up orchises, etc. I watered the garden and weeded. I did not leave home, in the expectation of Wm. and John, and sitting at work till after 11 o'clock I heard a foot go to the front of the house, turn round, and open the gate. It was William! After our first joy was over, we got some tea. We did not go to bed till 4 o'clock in the morning, so he had an opportunity of seeing our improvements. The birds were singing, and all looked fresh, though not gay. There was a greyness on earth and sky. We did not rise till near 10 in the morning. We were busy all day in writing letters to Coleridge, Montagu, Douglas, Richard.

Mr and Miss Simpson called in the evening, the little boy carried our letters to Ambleside. We walked with Mr and Miss S. home, on their return. The evening was cold and I was afraid of the toothach for William. We met John on our return home.

[*June*] 9th, *Monday*. In the morning W. cut down the winter cherry tree. I sowed French beans and weeded. A coronetted Landau went by, when we were sitting upon the sodded wall. The ladies (evidently Tourists) turned an eye of interest upon our little garden and cottage. We went to R. Newton's for pike floats and went round to Mr Gell's boat, and on the lake to fish. We caught nothing – it was extremely cold. The reeds and bullrushes or bullpipes of a tender soft green, making a plain whose surface moved with the wind. The reeds not yet tall. The lake clear to the bottom, but saw no fish. In the evening I stuck peas, watered the garden, and planted brocoli. Did not walk, for it was very cold. A poor girl called to beg, who had no work at home, and was going in search of it to Kendal. She slept in Mr Benson's, and went off after breakfast in the morning with 7d. and a letter to the Mayor of Kendal.

[*June*] 10th, *Tuesday*. A cold, yet sunshiny morning. John carried letters to Ambleside. I made tarts, pies, etc. Wm. stuck peas. After dinner he lay down. John not at home. I stuck peas alone. Molly washing. Cold showers with hail and rain, but at half past five, after a heavy rain, the lake became calm and very beautiful. Those parts of the water which were perfectly unruffled lay like green islands of various shapes. W. and I walked to Ambleside to seek lodgings for C. No letters. No papers. It was a very cold chearless evening. John had been fishing in Langdale and was gone to bed.

On Tuesday, May 27th, a very tall woman, tall much beyond the measure of tall women, called at the door. She had on a very long brown cloak, and a very white cap, without bonnet; her face was excessively brown, but it had plainly once been fair. She led a little bare-footed child about 2 years old by the hand, and said her husband, who was a tinker, was gone before with the other children. I gave her a piece of bread. Afterwards on my road to Ambleside, beside the bridge at Rydale, I saw her husband sitting by the roadside, his two asses feeding beside him, and the two young children at play upon the grass. The man did not beg. I passed on and about ¼ mile further I saw two boys before me, one about 10, the other about 8 years old, at play chasing a butterfly. They were wild figures, not very ragged, but without shoes and stockings; the hat of the elder was wreathed round with yellow flowers, the younger whose hat was only a rimless crown, had stuck it round with laurel leaves. They continued at play till I drew very near, and then they addressed me with the begging cant and the whining voice of sorrow. I said 'I served your mother this morning'. (The Boys were so like the woman who had called at the door that I could not be mistaken.) 'O!' says the elder, 'you could not serve my mother for she's dead, and my father's on at the next town – he's a potter.' I persisted in my assertion, and that I would give them nothing. Says the elder, 'Come, let's away', and

away they flew like lightning. They had however sauntered so long in their road that they did not reach
Ambleside before me, and I saw them go up to Matthew
Harrison's house with their wallet upon the elder's
shoulder, and creeping with a beggar's complaining foot.
On my return through Ambleside I met in the street the
mother driving her asses; in the two panniers of one
of which were the two little children, whom she was
chiding and threatening with a wand which she used to
drive her asses, while the little things hung in wantonness
over the pannier's edge. The woman had told me in the
morning that she was from Scotland, which her accent
fully proved, but that she had lived (I think) at Wigton,
that they could not keep a house and so they travelled.

June 11th, Wednesday. A very cold morning – we went on
the lake to set pike floats with John's fish. W. and J. went
first alone. Mr Simpson called, and I accompanied him
to the lake side. My Brothers and I again went upon the
water, and returned to dinner. We landed upon the
island where I saw the whitest hawthorn I have seen this
year, the generality of hawthorns are bloomless. I saw
wild roses in the hedges. Went to bed in the afternoon
and slept till after six – a threatening of the toothach.
Wm. and John went to the pike floats – they brought in
2 pikes. I sowed kidney-beans and spinnach. A cold
evening. Molly stuck the peas. I weeded a little. Did not
walk.

[June 16th,] Monday. Wm. and I went to Brathay by Little
Langdale and Collath and Skelleth. It was a warm mild

morning with threatening of rain. The vale of Little
Langdale looked bare and unlovely. Collath was wild
and interesting, from the peat carts and peat gatherers –
the valley all perfumed with the gale and wild thyme.
The woods about the waterfall veined with rich yellow
Broom.

A succession of delicious views from Skelleth to
Brathay. We met near Skelleth a pretty little boy with a
wallet over his shoulder. He came from Hawkshead and
was going to 'late a lock' of meal. He spoke gently and
without complaint. When I asked him if he got enough
to eat, he looked surprized, and said 'Nay'. He was 7
years old but seemed not more than 5. We drank tea at
Mr Ibbetson's, and returned by Ambleside. Lent 3 : 9 : 0
to the potter at Kendal. Met John on our return home at
about 10 o'clock. Saw a primrose in blossom.

[*June 21st,*] *Saturday*. In the morning W. and I went to
Ambleside to get his tooth drawn, and put in. A fine
clear morning but cold. W.'s tooth drawn with very little
pain – he slept till 3 o'clock. Young Mr S. drank tea and
supped with us. They fished in Rydale water and they
caught 2 small fishes – W. no bite – John 3. Miss Simpson
and 3 children called – I walked with them to Rydale.
The evening cold and clear and frosty but the wind was
falling as I returned – I staid at home about an hour and
then walked up the hill to Rydale lake. Grasmere looked
so beautiful that my heart was almost melted away. It
was quite calm, only spotted with sparkles of light. The
church visible. On our return all distant objects had faded
away – all but the hills. The reflection of the light bright

sky above Black Quarter was very solemn. Mr S. did not go till 12 o'clock.

[*June 22nd,*] *Sunday.* In the morning W. and I walked towards Rydale and up into the wood but finding it not very pleasant we returned – sauntered in the garden – a showery day. In the evening I planted a honeysuckle round the yew tree. In the evening we walked for letters – no letters. No news of Coleridge. Jimmy Benson came home drunk beside us.

[*June 23rd,*] *Monday.* Mr Simpson called in the morning. Tommy's Father dead. W. and I went into Langdale to fish. The morning was very cold. I sate at the foot of the lake, till my head ached with cold The view exquisitely beautiful, through a gate, and under a sycamore tree beside the first house going into Loughrigg. Elterwater looked barren, and the view from the church less beautiful than in winter. When W. went down to the water to fish, I lay under the [? wind], my head pillowed upon a mossy rock, and slept about 10 minutes, which relieved my headach. We ate our dinner together, and parted again. Wm. was afraid he had lost his line and sought me. An old man saw me just after I had crossed the stepping stones and was going through a copse – 'Ho, wherever were you going?' 'To Elterwater Bridge' – 'Why', says he, 'it's well I saw you; ye were gane to Little Langdale by Wrynose', and several other places which he ran over with a mixture of triumph, good-nature and wit – 'It's well I saw you or you'd ha' been lost.' The [? evening] grew very pleasant – We sate on the side of the hill looking to Elterwater. I was much tired and returned home to tea. W. went to fish for pike in Rydale. John came in when I had done tea, and he and I carried a jug of tea to William. We met him in the old road from Rydale. He drank his tea upon the turf. The setting sun threw a red purple light upon the rocks, and stone walls of Rydale, which gave them a most interesting and beautiful appearance.

[*June 24th,*] *Tuesday.* W. went to Ambleside. John walked out. I made tarts, etc. Mrs B. Simpson called and asked us to tea. I went to the view of Rydale, to meet William. John went to him – I returned. W. and I drank tea at Mr Simpson's. Brought down lemon-thyme, greens, etc. The old woman was very happy to see us, and we were so in the pleasure we gave. She was an affecting picture of patient disappointment, suffering under no particular affliction.

[*June 25th,*] *Wednesday.* A very rainy day. I made a shoe. Wm. and John went to fish in Langdale in the evening. I went above the house, and gathered flowers, which I planted, foxgloves, etc. On Sunday Mr and Mrs Coleridge and Hartley came. The day was very warm. We sailed to the foot of Loughrigg. They staid with us three weeks, and till the Thursday following, i.e. till the 23rd of July. On the Friday preceding their departure we drank tea at the island. The weather very delightful, and on the Sunday we made a great fire, and drank tea in Bainriggs with the Simpsons. I accompanied Mrs C. to Wytheburne, and returned with W. to tea at Mr Simpson's. It was excessively hot, but the day after, Friday 24th July, still hotter. All the morning I was engaged in unpacking our Somersetshire goods and in making pies. The house was a hot oven, but yet we could not bake the pies. I was so weary, I could not walk: so I went and sate with Wm. in the orchard. We had a delightful half-hour in the warm still evening.

[*July*] *26th, Saturday*. Still hotter. I sate with W. in the orchard all the morning, and made my shoes. In the afternoon from excessive heat I was ill in the headach and toothach and went to bed – I was refreshed with washing myself after I got up, but it was too hot to walk till near dark, and then I sate upon the wall finishing my shoes.

[*July*] *27th, Sunday*. Very warm. Molly ill. John bathed in the lake. I wrote out *Ruth* in the afternoon.

Ruth

> When Ruth was left half desolate,
> Her Father took another Mate;
> And Ruth, not seven years old,
> A slighted child, at her own will
> Went wandering over dale and hill,
> In thoughtless freedom, bold.
>
> And she had made a pipe of straw,
> And music from that pipe could draw
> Like sounds of winds and floods;

Had built a bower upon the green,
As if she from her birth had been
An infant of the woods.

Beneath her father's roof, alone
She seemed to live; her thoughts her own;
Herself her own delight;
Pleased with herself, nor sad, nor gay;
And, passing thus the live-long day,
She grew to woman's height.

There came a Youth from Georgia's shore –
A military casque he wore,
With splendid feathers drest;
He brought them from the Cherokees;
The feathers nodded in the breeze,
And made a gallant crest.

From Indian blood you deem him sprung:
But no! he spake the English tongue,
And bore a soldier's name;
And, when America was free
From battle and from jeopardy,
He 'cross the ocean came.

With hues of genius on his cheek
In finest tones the Youth could speak:
– While he was yet a boy,
The moon, the glory of the sun,
The streams that murmur as they run,
Had been his dearest joy.

He was a lovely Youth! I guess
The panther in the wilderness
Was not so fair as he;
And, when he chose to sport and play,
No dolphin ever was so gay
Upon the tropic sea.

Among the Indians he had fought,
And with him many tales he brought
Of pleasure and of fear;
Such tales as told to any maid
By such a Youth, in the green shade
Were perilous to hear.

He told of girls – a happy rout!
Who quit their fold with dance and shout,
Their pleasant Indian town,
To gather strawberries all day long;
Returning with a choral song
When daylight is gone down.

He spake of plants that hourly change
Their blossoms, through a boundless range
Of intermingling hues;
With budding, fading, faded flowers
They stand the wonder of the bowers
From morn to evening dews.

He told of the magnolia, spread
High as a cloud, high over head!
The cypress and her spire;

– Of flowers that with one scarlet gleam
Cover a hundred leagues, and seem
To set the hills on fire.

The Youth of green savannahs spake,
And many an endless, endless lake,
With all its fairy crowds
Of islands, that together lie
As quietly as spots of sky
Among the evening clouds.

'How pleasant,' then he said, 'it were
A fisher or a hunter there,
In sunshine or in shade
To wander with an easy mind;
And build a household fire, and find
A home in every glade!

'What days and what bright years! Ah me!
Our life were life indeed, with thee
So passed in quiet bliss,
And all the while,' said he, 'to know
That we were in a world of woe,
On such an earth as this!'

And then he sometimes interwove
Fond thoughts about a father's love;
'For there,' said he, 'are spun
Around the heart such tender ties,
That our own children to our eyes
Are dearer than the sun.

'Sweet Ruth! and could you go with me
My helpmate in the woods to be,
Our shed at night to rear;
Or run, my own adopted bride,
A sylvan huntress at my side!
And drive the flying deer!

'Beloved Ruth!' – No more he said,
The wakeful Ruth at midnight shed
A solitary tear:
She thought again – and did agree
With him to sail across the sea,
And drive the flying deer.

'And now, as fitting is and right,
We in the church our faith will plight,
A husband and a wife.'
Even so they did; and I may say
That to sweet Ruth that happy day
Was more than human life.

Through dream and vision did she sink,
Delighted all the while to think
That on those lonesome floods,
And green savannahs, she would share
His board with lawful joy, and bear
His name in the wild woods.

But, as you have before been told,
This Stripling, sportive, gay and bold,
And, with his dancing crest,

So beautiful, through savage lands
Had roamed about, with vagrant bands
Of Indians in the West.

The wind, the tempest roaring high,
The tumult of a tropic sky,
Might well be dangerous food
For him, a Youth to whom was given
So much of earth – so much of heaven,
And such impetuous blood.

Whatever in those climes he found
Irregular in sight or sound
Did to his mind impart
A kindred impulse, seemed allied
To his own powers, and justified
The workings of his heart.

Nor less, to feed voluptuous thought,
The beauteous forms of nature wrought,
Fair trees and gorgeous flowers;
The breezes their own languor lent;
The stars had feelings, which they sent
Into those favoured bowers.

Yet, in his worst pursuits, I ween
That sometimes there did intervene
Pure hopes of high intent:
For passions linked to forms so fair
And stately, needs must have their share
Of noble sentiment.

But ill he lived, much evil saw,
With men to whom no better law
Nor better life was known;
Deliberately, and undeceived,
Those wild men's vices he received,
And gave them back his own.

His genius and his moral frame
Were thus impaired, and he became
The slave of low desires:
A Man who without self-control
Would seek what the degraded soul
Unworthily admires.

And yet he with no feigned delight
Had wooed the Maiden, day and night
Had loved her, night and morn:
What could he less than love a Maid
Whose heart with so much nature played?
So kind and so forlorn!

Sometimes, most earnestly, he said,
'O Ruth! I have been worse than dead;
False thoughts, thoughts bold and vain,
Encompassed me on every side
When I, in confidence and pride,
Had crossed the Atlantic main.

'Before me shone a glorious world –
Fresh as a banner bright, unfurled
To music suddenly:

I looked upon those hills and plains,
And seemed as if let loose from chains,
To live at liberty.

'No more of this; for now, by thee
Dear Ruth! more happily set free
With nobler zeal I burn;
My soul from darkness is released,
Like the whole sky when to the east
The morning doth return.'

Full soon that better mind was gone;
No hope, no wish remained, not one, –
They stirred him now no more;
New objects did new pleasure give
And once again he wished to live
As lawless as before.

Meanwhile, as thus with him it fared,
They for the voyage were prepared,
And went to the sea-shore,
But, when they thither came the Youth
Deserted his poor Bride, and Ruth
Could never find him more.

God help thee, Ruth! – Such pains she had,
That she in half a year was mad,
And in a prison housed;
And there, with many a doleful song
Made of wild words, her cup of wrong
She fearfully caroused.

Yet sometimes milder hours she knew,
Nor wanted sun, nor rain, nor dew,
Nor pastimes of the May;
– They all were with her in her cell;
And a clear brook with cheerful knell
Did o'er the pebbles play.

When Ruth three seasons thus had lain,
There came a respite to her pain;
She from her prison fled;
But of the Vagrant none took thought;
And where it liked her best she sought
Her shelter and her bread.

Among the fields she breathed again:
The master-current of her brain
Ran permanent and free;
And, coming to the Banks of Tone,
There did she rest; and dwell alone
Under the greenwood tree.

The engines of her pain, the tools
That shaped her sorrow, rocks and pools,
And airs that gently stir
The vernal leaves – she loved them still;
Nor ever taxed them with the ill
Which had been done to her.

A Barn her winter bed supplies;
But, till the warmth of summer skies
And summer days is gone,

(And all do in this tale agree)
She sleeps beneath the greenwood tree,
And other home hath none.

An innocent life, yet far astray!
And Ruth will, long before her day,
Be broken down and old:
Sore aches she needs must have! but less
Of mind, than body's wretchedness,
From damp, and rain, and cold.

If she is prest by want of food,
She from her dwelling in the wood
Repairs to a road-side;
And there she begs at one steep place
Where up and down with easy pace
The horsemen-travellers ride.

That oaten pipe of hers is mute,
Or thrown away; but with a flute
Her loneliness she cheers:
This flute, made of a hemlock stalk,
At evening in his homeward walk
The Quantock woodman hears.

I, too, have passed her on the hills
Setting her little water-mills
By spouts and fountains wild –
Such small machinery as she turned
Ere she had wept, ere she had mourned,
A young and happy Child!

Farewell! and when thy days are told,
Ill-fated Ruth, in hallowed mould
Thy corpse shall buried be,
For thee a funeral bell shall ring,
And all the congregation sing
A Christian psalm for thee.

In the morning, I read Mr Knight's *Landscape*. After tea we rowed down to Loughrigg Fell, visited the white foxglove, gathered wild strawberries, and walked up to view Rydale. We lay a long time looking at the lake: the shores all embrowned with the scorching sun. The ferns were turning yellow, that is, here and there one was quite turned. We walked round by Benson's wood home. The lake was now most still, and reflected the beautiful yellow and blue and purple and grey colours of the sky. We heard a strange sound in the Bainriggs wood, as we were floating on the water; it *seemed* in the wood, but it must have been above it, for presently we saw a raven very high above us. It called out, and the dome of the sky seemed to echo the sound. It called again and again as it flew onwards, and the mountains gave back the sound, seeming as if from their center; a musical bell-like answering to the bird's hoarse voice. We heard both the call of the bird, and the echo, after we could see him no longer.

Passage from the Excursion, Book IV

. . . and often, at the hour
When issue forth the first pale stars, is heard
Within the circuit of this fabric huge,
One voice – the solitary raven, flying
Athwart the concave of the dark blue dome,
Unseen, perchance above all power of sight –
An iron knell! with echoes from afar
Faint – and still fainter – as the cry, with which
The wanderer accompanies her flight
Through the calm region, fades upon the ear,
Diminishing by distance till it seemed
To expire; yet from the abyss is caught again,
And yet again recovered!

[*July 28th,*] *Monday Morning.* Received a letter from Coleridge enclosing one from Mr Davy about the *Lyrical Ballads.* Intensely hot. I made pies in the morning. William went into the wood, and altered his poems. In the evening it was so very warm that I was too much tired to walk.

[*July 29th,*] *Tuesday.* Still very hot. We gathered peas for dinner. We walked up in the evening to find out Hewetson's cottage but it was too dark. I was sick and weary.

[*July 30th,*] *Wednesday.* Gathered peas for Mrs Simpson – John and I walked up with them – very hot – Wm. had intended going to Keswick. I was obliged to lie down after dinner from excessive heat and headach. The evening excessively beautiful – a rich reflection of the moon, the moonlight, clouds and the hills, and from the Rays gap a huge rainbow pillar. We sailed upon the lake till it was 10 o'clock.

[*July 31st,*] *Thursday.* All the morning I was busy copying poems. Gathered peas, and in the afternoon Coleridge came, very hot; he brought the 2nd volume of the Anthology. The men went to bathe, and we afterwards sailed down to Loughrigg. Read poems on the water, and let the boat take its own course. We walked a long time upon Loughrigg. I returned in the grey twilight. The moon just setting as we reached home.

August 1st, Friday. In the morning I copied *The Brothers.* Coleridge and Wm. went down to the lake. They returned, and we all went together to Mary Point, where we sate in the breeze and the shade, and read Wm.'s poems. Altered *The Whirlblast,* etc.

> A whirl-blast from behind the hill
> Rushed o'er the wood with startling sound;
> Then – all at once the air was still,
> And showers of hailstones pattered round.
> Where leafless oaks towered high above,
> I sat within an undergrove
> Of tallest hollies, tall and green;
> A fairer bower was never seen.

From year to year the spacious floor
With withered leaves is covered o'er,
And all the year the bower is green.
But see! where'er the hailstones drop
The withered leaves all skip and hop;
There's not a breeze – no breath of air –
Yet here, and there, and everywhere
Along the floor, beneath the shade
By those embowering hollies made,
The leaves in myriads jump and spring,
As if with pipes and music rare
Some Robin Good-fellow were there,
And all those leaves, in festive glee,
Were dancing to the minstrelsy.

August 17th, Sunday. Came home. Dined in Borrowdale. A rainy morning, but a fine evening – saw the Bristol prison and Bassenthwaite at the same time – Wm. read us *The Seven Sisters* on a stone.

The Seven Sisters or, the Solitude of Binnorie

I

Seven Daughters had Lord Archibald,
All children of one mother:
You could not say in one short day
What love they bore each other.
A garland, of seven lilies, wrought!
Seven Sisters that together dwell;

But he, bold Knight as ever fought,
Their Father, took of them no thought,
He loved the wars so well.
Sing, mournfully, oh! mournfully,
The solitude of Binnorie!

II

Fresh blows the wind, a western wind,
And from the shores of Erin,
Across the wave, a Rover brave
To Binnorie is steering:
Right onward to the Scottish strand
The gallant ship is borne;
The warriors leap upon the land,
And hark! the Leader of the band
Hath blown his bugle horn.
Sing, mournfully, oh! mournfully,
The solitude of Binnorie.

III

Beside a grotto of their own,
With boughs above them closing,
The Seven are laid, and in the shade
They lie like dawns reposing.
But now, upstarting with affright
At noise of man and steed,
Away they fly to left, to right –
Of your fair household, Father-Knight,
Methinks you take small heed!
Sing, mournfully, oh! mournfully,
The solitude of Binnorie.

IV

Away the seven fair Campbells fly,
And, over hill and hollow,
With menace proud, and insult loud,
The youthful Rovers follow.
Cried they, 'Your Father loves to roam:
Enough for him to find
The empty house when he comes home;
For us your yellow ringlets comb,
For us be fair and kind!'
Sing, mournfully, oh! mournfully,
The solitude of Binnorie.

V

Some close behind, some side to side,
Like clouds in stormy weather;
They run, and cry, 'Nay, let us die,
And let us die together.'
A lake was near; the shore was steep;
There never foot had been;
They ran, and with a desperate leap
Together plunged into the deep,
Nor ever more were seen.
Sing, mournfully, oh! mournfully,
The solitude of Binnorie.

VI

The stream that flows out of the lake,
As through the glen it rambles,
Repeats a moan o'er moss and stone,
For those seven lovely Campbells.

Dorothy and William Wordsworth

Seven little Islands, green and bare,
Have risen from out the deep:
The fishers say, those sisters fair,
By faeries all are buried there,
And there together sleep.
Sing, mournfully, oh! mournfully,
The solitude of Binnorie.

2

'And She who dwells with me, whom I have loved
With such communion, that no place on earth
Can ever be a solitude to me,
Hath to this lonely Summit given my Name.'

From *Poems on the Naming of Places*, III

[*August 21st,*] *Thursday*. Read *Wallenstein* and sent it off –
worked in the morning – walked with John round the
two lakes – gathered white fox-glove seeds and found
Wm. in Bainriggs at our return.

[*August*] *22nd, Friday*. Very cold. Baking in the morning,
gathered pea seeds and took up – lighted a fire upstairs.
Walked as far as Rydale with John intending to have
gone on to Ambleside, but we found the papers at Rydale
– Wm. walking in the wood all the time. John and he
went out after our return – I mended stockings. Wind
very high shaking the corn.

[*August*] *23rd, Saturday*. A very fine morning. Wm. was
composing all the morning. I shelled peas, gathered
beans, and worked in the garden till ½ past 12. Then
walked with Wm. in the wood. The gleams of sunshine,

and the stirring trees, and gleaming boughs, chearful lake, most delightful. After dinner we walked to Ambleside – showery – went to see Mr Partridge's house. Came home by Clappersgate. We had intended going by Rydale woods, but it was cold – I was not well, and tired. Got tea immediately and had a fire. Did not reach home till 7 o'clock – mended stockings and Wm. read *Peter Bell*. He read us the poem of *Joanna*, beside the Rothay by the roadside.

To Joanna

Amid the smoke of cities did you pass
The time of early youth; and there you learned,
From years of quiet industry, to love
The living Beings by your own fireside,
With such a strong devotion, that your heart
Is slow to meet the sympathies of them
Who look upon the hills with tenderness,
And make dear friendships with the streams and groves.
Yet we, who are transgressors in this kind,
Dwelling retired in our simplicity
Among the woods and fields, we love you well,
Joanna! and I guess, since you have been
So distant from us now for two long years,
That you will gladly listen to discourse,
However trivial, if you thence be taught
That they, with whom you once were happy, talk
Familiarly of you and of old times.

While I was seated, now some ten days past,
Beneath those lofty firs, that overtop
Their ancient neighbour, the old steeple-tower,
The Vicar from his gloomy house hard by
Came forth to greet me; and when he had asked,
'How fares Joanna, that wild-hearted Maid!
And when will she return to us?' he paused;
And, after short exchange of village news,
He with grave looks demanded, for what cause,
Reviving obsolete idolatry,
I, like a Runic Priest, in characters
Of formidable size had chiselled out
Some uncouth name upon the native rock,
Above the Rotha, by the forest-side.
– Now, by those dear immunities of heart
Engendered between malice and true love,
I was not loth to be so catechised,
And this was my reply:– 'As it befell,
One summer morning we had walked abroad
At break of day, Joanna and myself.
– 'Twas that delightful season when the broom,
Full-flowered, and visible on every steep,
Along the copses runs in veins of gold.
Our pathway led us on to Rotha's banks;
And when we came in front of that tall rock
That eastward looks, I there stopped short – and stood
Tracing the lofty barrier with my eye
From base to summit; such delight I found
To note in shrub and tree, in stone and flower
That intermixture of delicious hues,
Along so vast a surface, all at once,

In one impression, by connecting force
Of their own beauty, imaged in the heart.
– When I had gazed perhaps two minutes' space,
Joanna, looking in my eyes, beheld
That ravishment of mine, and laughed aloud.
The Rock, like something starting from a sleep
Took up the Lady's voice, and laughed again;
That ancient Woman seated on Helm-crag
Was ready with her cavern; Hammar-scar,
And the tall Steep of Silver-how, sent forth
A noise of laughter; southern Loughrigg heard,
And Fairfield answered with a mountain tone;
Helvellyn far into the clear blue sky
Carried the Lady's voice, – old Skiddaw blew
His speaking-trumpet; – back out of the clouds
Of Glaramara southward came the voice;
And Kirkstone tossed it from his misty head.
– Now whether (said I to our cordial Friend,
Who in the hey-day of astonishment
Smiled in my face) this were in simple truth
A work accomplished by the brotherhood
Of ancient mountains, or my ear was touched
With dreams and visionary impulses
To me alone imparted, sure I am
That there was a loud uproar in the hills.
And, while we both were listening; to my side
The fair Joanna drew, as if she wished
To shelter from some object of her fear.
– And hence, long afterwards, when eighteen moons
Were wasted, as I chanced to walk alone
Beneath this rock, at sunrise, on a calm

And silent morning, I sat down, and there,
In memory of affections old and true,
I chiselled out in those rude characters
Joanna's name deep in the living stone:
And I, and all who dwell by my fireside,
Have called the lovely rock, JOANNA'S ROCK.'

[*August*] *26th, Tuesday*. We walked in the evening to Ambleside – Wm. not quite well. I bought sacking for the mattrass. A very fine solemn evening. The wind blew very free from the islands at Rydale. We went on the other side of Rydale, and sate a long time looking at the mountains, which were all black at Grasmere, and very bright in Rydale; Grasmere exceedingly dark, and Rydale of a light yellow green.

[*August*] *27th, Wednesday*. In the morning Wm. walked. We walked along the shore of the lake in the evening, went over into Langdale and down to Loughrigg Tarn – a very fine evening calm and still.

[*August 28th,*] *Thursday*. Still very fine weather. I baked bread and cakes. In the evening we walked round the Lake by Rydale. Mr Simpson came to fish.

[*August 29th,*] *Friday Evening*. We walked to Rydale to inquire for letters. We walked over the hill by the fir-grove. I sate upon a rock, and observed a flight of swallows gathering together high above my head. They flew towards Rydale. We walked through the wood over the stepping-stones. The lake of Rydale very beautiful, partly still. John and I left Wm. to compose an inscription – that about the path. We had a very fine walk by the gloomy lake. There was a curious yellow reflection in the water, as of corn fields. There was no light in the clouds from which it appeared to come.

The inscription referred to above is now thought to be six lines entitled 'The Orchard Pathway' which W. originally intended to be the motto for the whole group On the Naming of Places.

The Orchard Pathway

> Orchard Pathway, to and fro,
> Ever with thee, did I go,
> Weaving Verses, a huge store!
> These and many hundreds more,
> And, in memory of the same,
> This little lot shall bear thy name!

August 30th, Saturday Morning. I was baking bread, pies and dinner. It was very warm. William finished his Inscription of the Pathway, then walked in the wood; and when John returned, he sought him, and they bathed together. I read a little of Boswell's *Life of Johnson*. I had a headach and went to lie down in the orchard. I was roused by a shout that Anthony Harrison was come. We sate in the orchard till tea time. Drank tea early, and rowed down the lake which was stirred by breezes. We looked at Rydale, which was soft, chearful and beautiful. We then went to peep into Langdale. The Pikes were very grand. We walked back to the view of Rydale, which was now a dark mirror. We rowed home over a lake still as glass, and then went to George Mackareth's to hire a horse for John. A fine moonlight night. The beauty of the moon was startling, as it rose to us over Loughrigg Fell. We returned to supper at 10 o'clock. Thomas Ashburner brought us our 8th cart of coals since May 17th.

[*August*] *31st, Sunday*. Anthony Harrison and John left us at ½ past seven – a very fine morning. A great deal of corn is cut in the vale, and the whole prospect, though not tinged with a general autumnal yellow, yet softened down into a mellowness of colouring, which seems to impart softness to the forms of hills and mountains. At 11 o'clock Coleridge came, when I was walking in the still clear moonshine in the garden. He came over Helvellyn. Wm. was gone to bed, and John also, worn out with his ride round Coniston. We sate and chatted till ½ past three, W. in his dressing gown. Coleridge read us a part of *Christabel*. Talked much about the mountains, etc. etc. Miss Thrale's – Losh's opinion of Southey – the first of poets.

September 1st, Monday Morning. We walked in the wood by the lake. W. read *Joanna*, and the *Firgrove*, to Coleridge. They bathed. The morning was delightful, with somewhat of an autumnal freshness. After dinner, Coleridge discovered a rock-seat in the orchard. Cleared away the brambles. Coleridge obliged to go to bed after tea. John and I followed Wm. up the hill, and then returned to go to Mr Simpson's. We borrowed some bottles for bottling rum. The evening somewhat frosty and grey, but very pleasant. I broiled Coleridge a mutton chop, which he ate in bed. Wm. was gone to bed. I chatted with John and Coleridge till near 12.

> When, to the attractions of the busy world
> Preferring studious leisure, I had chosen
> A habitation in this peaceful Vale,
> Sharp season followed of continual storm
> In deepest winter; and, from week to week,
> Pathway, and lane, and public road, were clogged
> With frequent showers of snow. Upon a hill
> At a short distance from my cottage, stands
> A stately Fir-grove, whither I was wont
> To hasten, for I found, beneath the roof
> Of that perennial shade, a cloistral place
> Of refuge, with an unincumbered floor.
> Here, in safe covert, on the shallow snow,
> And, sometimes, on a speck of visible earth,
> The redbreast near me hopped; nor was I loth
> To sympathise with vulgar coppice birds
> That, for protection from the nipping blast,
> Hither repaired. – A single beech-tree grew
> Within this grove of firs! and, on the fork
> Of that one beech, appeared a thrush's nest;
> A last year's nest, conspicuously built
> At such small elevation from the ground
> As gave sure sign that they, who in that house
> Of nature and of love had made their home
> Amid the fir-trees, all the summer long

Dwelt in a tranquil spot. And oftentimes,
A few sheep, stragglers from some mountain-flock,
Would watch my motions with suspicious stare,
From the remotest outskirts of the grove, –
Some nook where they had made their final stand,
Huddling together from two fears – the fear
Of me and of the storm. Full many an hour
Here did I lose. But in this grove the trees
Had been so thickly planted, and had thriven
In such perplexed and intricate array,
That vainly did I seek, beneath their stems
A length of open space, where to and fro
My feet might move without concern or care;
And, baffled thus, though earth from day to day
Was fettered, and the air by storm disturbed,
I ceased the shelter to frequent, – prized,
Less than I wished to prize, that calm recess.

The snows dissolved, and genial Spring returned
To clothe the fields with verdure. Other haunts
Meanwhile were mine; till, one bright April day,
By chance retiring from the glare of noon
To this forsaken covert, there I found
A hoary pathway traced between the trees,
And winding on with such an easy line
Along a natural opening, that I stood
Much wondering how I could have sought in vain
For what was now so obvious. To abide,
For an allotted interval of ease,
Under my cottage-roof, had gladly come
From the wild sea a cherished Visitant;

And with the sight of this same path – begun,
Begun and ended, in the shady grove,
Pleasant conviction flashed upon my mind
That, to this opportune recess allured,
He had surveyed it with a finer eye,
A heart more wakeful; and had worn the track
By pacing here, unwearied and alone,
In that habitual restlessness of foot
That haunts the Sailor measuring o'er and o'er
His short domain upon the vessel's deck,
While she pursues her course through the dreary sea.

When thou hadst quitted Esthwaite's pleasant shore,
And taken thy first leave of those green hills
And rocks that were the play-ground of thy youth,
Year followed year, my Brother! and we two,
Conversing not, knew little in what mould
Each other's mind was fashioned; and at length,
When once again we met in Grasmere Vale,
Between us there was little other bond
Than common feelings of fraternal love.
But thou, a Schoolboy, to the sea hadst carried
Undying recollections! Nature there
Was with thee; she, who loved us both, she still
Was with thee; and even so didst thou become
A *silent* Poet; from the solitude
Of the vast sea didst bring a watchful heart
Still couchant, an inevitable ear,
And an eye practised like a blind man's touch.
– Back to the joyless Ocean thou art gone;
Nor from this vestige of thy musing hours

Could I withhold thy honoured name, – and now
I love the fir-grove with a perfect love.
Thither do I withdraw when cloudless suns
Shine hot, or wind blows troublesome and strong;
And there I sit at evening, when the steep
Of Silver-how, and Grasmere's peaceful lake,
And one green island, gleam between the stems
Of the dark firs, a visionary scene!
And, while I gaze upon the spectacle
Of clouded splendour, on this dream-like sight
Of solemn loveliness, I think on thee,
My Brother, and on all which thou hast lost.
Nor seldom, if I rightly guess, while Thou,
Muttering the verses which I muttered first
Among the mountains, through the midnight watch
Art pacing thoughtfully the vessel's deck
In some far region, here, while o'er my head,
At every impulse of the moving breeze,
The fir-grove murmurs with a sea-like sound,
Alone I tread this path; – for aught I know,
Timing my steps to thine; and, with a store
Of undistinguishable sympathies,
Mingling most earnest wishes for the day
When we, and others whom we love, shall meet
A second time, in Grasmere's happy Vale.

NOTE. – This wish was not granted; the lamented Person not long after perished by shipwreck, in discharge of his duty as Commander of the Honourable East India Company's Vessel, the *Earl of Abergavenny*.

*

[*September*] *2nd, Tuesday*. In the morning they all went to
Stickle Tarn. A very fine, warm, sunny, beautiful morning. I baked a pie etc. for dinner – Little Sally was with
me. The fair-day. Miss Simpson and Mr came down to
tea – we walked to the fair. There seemed very few
people and very few stalls, yet I believe there were many
cakes and much beer sold. My brothers came home to
dinner at 6 o'clock. We drank tea immediately after by
candlelight. It was a lovely moonlight night. We talked
much about a house on Helvellyn. The moonlight shone
only upon the village. It did not eclipse the village lights,
and the sound of dancing and merriment came along the
still air. I walked with Coleridge and Wm. up the lane
and by the church, and then lingered with Coleridge in
the garden. John and Wm. were both gone to bed, and
all the lights out.

September 3rd, Wednesday. Coleridge, Wm., and John
went from home, to go upon Helvellyn with Mr Simpson. They set out after breakfast. I accompanied them
up near the blacksmith's. A fine coolish morning. I ironed
till ½ past 3 – now very hot – I then went to a funeral
at John Dawson's. About 10 men and 4 women. Bread,
cheese, and ale. They talked sensibly and chearfully
about common things. The dead person, 56 years of age,
buried by the parish. The coffin was neatly lettered and
painted black, and covered with a decent cloth. They set
the corpse down at the door; and, while we stood within
the threshold, the men with their hats off sang with
decent and solemn countenances a verse of a funeral
psalm. The corpse was then borne down the hill, and

they sang till they had passed the Town-End. I was affected to tears while we stood in the house, the coffin lying before me. There were no near kindred, no children. When we got out of the dark house the sun was shining, and the prospect looked so divinely beautiful as I never saw it. It seemed more sacred than I had ever seen it, and yet more allied to human life. The green fields, neighbours of the churchyard, were as green as possible; and, with the brightness of the sunshine, looked quite gay. I thought she was going to a quiet spot, and I could not help weeping very much. When we came to the bridge, they began to sing again, and stopped during four lines before they entered the churchyard. The priest met us – he did not look as a man ought to do on such an occasion – I had seen him half-drunk the day before in a pot-house. Before we came with the corpse one of the company observed he wondered what sort of cue our Parson would be in! N.B. It was the day after the Fair. I had not finished ironing till 7 o'clock. The wind was now high and I did not walk – writing my journal now at 8 o'clock. Wm. and John came home at 10 o'clock.

[*September*] *9th, Tuesday Morning*. Mr Marshall came – he dined with us. My Brothers walked with him round the lakes after dinner – windy – we went to the island. W. and I after to tea. John and I went to the B. quarter, before supper went to seek a horse at Dawson's, Firgrove. After supper, talked of Wm.'s poems.

Sept[*ember*] *10th, Wednesday*. After breakfast Mr Marshall, Wm. and John went on horseback to Keswick – I wrote to Mrs Marshall – a fine autumn day. I had a fire. Paid Mr Bonsfield 8:2:11. After tea walked with French Beans to Mr Simpson's – went up to the Forest side above a deserted house – sat till twilight came on. Mr and Miss S. came down with me and supped.

[*September*] *11th, Thursday*. All the morning mending white gown – washed my head – Molly washing. Drank tea at Mr Simpson's. Found Wm. at home at my return – he was unable to go on with Mr Marshall and parted from him in Borrowdale. Made tea after my return.

Sept[*ember*] *12th, Friday*. I worked in the morning. Cut my thumb. Walked in the Firgrove before dinner – after dinner sate under the trees in the orchard – a rainy morning, but very fine afternoon. Miss Simpson called for my packing needle. The Fern of the mountains now spreads yellow veins among the trees, the coppice wood turns brown. William observed some affecting little things in Borrowdale. A decayed house with this inscription [*blank space in MS.*] in the Church yard, the tall silent rocks seen thro' the broken windows. A kind of rough column put upon the gravel end of a house, with a ball stone, smooth from the river placed upon it for an ornament. Near it one stone like it upon an old mansion, carefully hewn.

September 13th, Saturday Morning. William writing his Preface – did not walk. Jones, and Mr Palmer came to tea. We walked with them to Borricks – a lovely evening, but the air frosty – worked when I returned home. Wm. walked out. John came home from Mr Marshall. Sent back word to Mrs Clarkson.

[*September*] *29th, on Monday*. John left us. Wm. and I parted with him in sight of Ulswater. It was a fine day, showery, but with sunshine and fine clouds. Poor fellow, my heart was right sad. I could not help thinking we should see him again, because he was only going to Penrith.

It is this parting which is described in the poem Wordsworth wrote after hearing of his brother's death.

Elegiac Verses

In Memory of my Brother
John Wordsworth.

Commander of the E.I. Company's Ship
the *Earl of Abergavenny*, in
which he perished by calamitous
shipwreck, Feb. 6, 1805.

I

The Sheep-boy whistled loud, and lo!
That instant, startled by the shock,
The Buzzard mounted from the rock
Deliberate and slow:

Lord of the air, he took his flight;
Oh! could he on that woeful night
Have lent his wing, my Brother dear,
For one poor moment's space to Thee,
And all who struggled with the Sea,
When safety was so near.

II

Thus in the weakness of my heart
I spoke (but let that pang be still)
When rising from the rock at will,
I saw the Bird depart.
And let me calmly bless the Power
That meets me in this unknown Flower.
Affecting type of him I mourn!
With calmness suffer and believe,
And grieve, and know that I must grieve,
Not cheerless, though forlorn.

III

Here did we stop; and here looked round
While each into himself descends,
For that last thought of parting Friends
That is not to be found.
Hidden was Grasmere Vale from sight,
Our home and his, his heart's delight,
His quiet heart's selected home.
But time before him melts away,
And he hath feeling of a day
Of blessedness to come.

IV

Full soon in sorrow did I weep,
Taught that the mutual hope was dust,
In sorrow, but for higher trust,
How miserably deep!
All vanished in a single word,
A breath, a sound, and scarcely heard:
Sea – Ship – drowned – Shipwreck – so it came,
The meek, the brave, the good, was gone;
He who had been our living John
Was nothing but a name.

V

That was indeed a parting! oh,
Glad am I, glad that it is past;
For there were some on whom it cast
Unutterable woe.
But they as well as I have gains; –
From many a humble source, to pains
Like these, there comes a mild release;
Even here I feel it, even this Plant
Is in its beauty ministrant
To comfort and to peace.

VI

He would have loved thy modest grace,
Meek Flower! To Him I would have said,
'It grows upon its native bed
Beside our Parting-place;
There, cleaving to the ground, it lies

With multitude of purple eyes,
Spangling a cushion green like moss;
But we will see it, joyful tide!
Some day, to see it in its pride,
The mountain will we cross.'

VII
– Brother and Friend, if verse of mine
Have power to make thy virtues known,
Here let a monumental Stone
Stand – sacred as a Shrine;
And to the few who pass this way,
Traveller or Shepherd, let it say,
Long as these mighty rocks endure, –
Oh do not Thou too fondly brood,
Although deserving of all good,
On any earthly hope however pure!

September 30th, on Tuesday. Charles Lloyd dined with us.
We walked homewards with him after dinner. It rained
very hard. Rydale was extremely wild, and we had a
fine walk. We sate quietly and comfortably by the fire.
I wrote the last sheet of Notes and Preface.

October 1st, Wednesday. A fine morning, a showery night.
The lake still in the morning; in the forenoon flashing
light from the beams of the sun, as it was ruffled by the
wind. We corrected the last sheet.

October 2nd, Thursday. A very rainy morning. We walked
after dinner to observe the torrents. I followed Wm. to

Rydale, he afterwards went to Butterlip How. I came home to receive the Lloyds. They walked with us to see Churnmilk force and the Black quarter. The Black Quarter looked marshy, and the general prospect was cold, but the Force was very grand. The Lichens are now coming out a fresh, I carried home a collection in the afternoon. We had a pleasant conversation about the manners of the rich – avarice, inordinate desires, and the effeminacy, unnaturalness, and the unworthy objects of education. After the Lloyds were gone we walked – a showery evening. The moonlight lay upon the hills like snow.

October 3rd, Friday. Very rainy all the morning. Little Sally learning to mark. Wm. walked to Ambleside after dinner, I went with him part of the way. He talked much about the object of his essay for the second volume of 'L.B.' I returned expecting the Simpsons – they did not come. I should have met Wm. but my teeth ached and it was showery and late – he returned after 10. Amos Cottle's death in the *Morning Post*. Wrote to S. Lowthian.

N.B. When Wm. and I returned from accompanying Jones, we met an old man almost double. He had on a coat, thrown over his shoulders, above his waistcoat and coat. Under this he carried a bundle, and had an apron on and a night-cap. His face was interesting. He had dark eyes and a long nose. John, who afterwards met him at Wytheburn, took him for a Jew. He was of Scotch parents, but had been born in the army. He had had a wife, and 'a good woman, and it pleased God to bless us with ten children'. All these were dead but one, of whom he had not heard for many years, a sailor. His trade was to gather leeches, but now leeches are scarce, and he had not strength for it. He lived by begging, and was making his way to Carlisle, where he should buy a few godly books to sell. He said leeches were very scarce, partly owing to this dry season, but many years they had been scarce – he supposed it owing to their being much sought after, that they did not breed fast, and were of slow growth. Leeches were formerly 2s 6d. [per] 100; they are now 30s. He had been hurt in driving a cart, his leg broke, his body driven over, his skull fractured. He felt no pain till he recovered from his first insensibility. It was then late in the evening, when the light was just going away.

October 4th, 1800, Saturday. A very rainy, or rather showery and gusty, morning; for often the sun shines. Thomas Ashburner could not go to Keswick. Read a part of Lamb's Play. The language is often very beautiful, but too imitative in particular phrases, words, etc. The characters, except Margaret's, unintelligible, and, except Margaret's, do not show themselves in action. Coleridge came in while we were at dinner, very wet – we talked till 12 o'clock. He had sate up all the night before, writing Essays for the newspaper. His youngest child had been very ill in convulsion fits. Exceedingly delighted with the second part of *Christabel*.

October 5th, Sunday Morning. Coleridge read a 2nd time *Christabel*; we had increasing pleasure. A delicious morning. Wm. and I were employed all the morning in writing an addition to the Preface. Wm. went to bed, very ill after working after dinner. Coleridge and I walked to Ambleside after dark with the letter. Returned to tea at 9 o'clock. Wm. still in bed, and very ill. Silver How in both lakes.

[*October 6th,*] *Monday*. A rainy day. Coleridge intending to go, but did not get off. We walked after dinner to Rydale. After tea read *The Pedlar*. Determined not to print *Christabel* with the L.B.

[*October 7th,*] *Tuesday*. Coleridge went off at eleven o'clock. I went as far as Mrs Simpson's. Returned with Mary. She drank tea here. I was very ill in the evening at the Simpsons – went to bed – supped there. Returned with Miss S. and Mrs J. – heavy showers. Found Wm. at home. I was still weak and unwell – went to bed immediately.

[*October 8th,*] *Wednesday*. A threatening bad morning – We dried the linen. Frequent threatening of showers. Received a £5 note from Montagu. Wm. walked to Rydale. I copied a part of *The Beggar* in the morning. I was not quite well in the evening, therefore I did not walk – Wm. walked. A very mild moonlight night. Glow-worms everywhere.

[*October 9th,*] *Thursday*. I was ironing all the day till tea time. Very rainy. Wm. and I walked in the evening, intending to go to Lloyd's, but it came on so very rainy that we were obliged to shelter at Fleming's. A grand

Ball at Rydale. After sitting some time we went homewards and were again caught by a shower and sheltered
under the sycamores at the boat-house – a very cold
snowlike rain. A man called in a soldier's dress – he was
thirty years old, of Cockermouth, had lost a leg and thigh
in battle, was going to his home. He could earn more
money in travelling with his ass than at home.

October 10th, Friday. In the morning when I arose the
mists were hanging over the opposite hills, and the tops
of the highest hills were covered with snow. There was
a most lovely combination at the head of the vale of
the yellow autumnal hills wrapped in sunshine, and
overhung with partial mists, the green and yellow trees,
and the distant snow-topped mountains. It was a most
heavenly morning. The Cockermouth traveller came
with thread, hardware, mustard, etc. She is very healthy;
has travelled over the mountains these thirty years. She
does not mind the storms, if she can keep her goods dry.
Her husband will not travel with an ass, because it is the
tramper's badge; she would have one to relieve her from
the weary load. She was going to Ulverston, and was to
return to Ambleside Fair. After I had finished baking I
went out with Wm., Mrs Jameson and Miss Simpson
towards Rydale – the fern among the rocks exquisitely
beautiful. We turned home and walked to Mr Gell's.
After dinner Wm. went to bed – I read Southey's letter.
Miss Simpson and Mrs Jameson came to tea. After tea
we went to Lloyd's – a fine evening as we went, but
rained in returning – we were wet – found them not at
home. I wrote to Mrs Clarkson. Sent off *The Beggar*, etc.,

by Thomas Ashburner who went to fetch our 9th cart
of coals. William sat up after me, writing *Point Rash
Judgment*.

> A narrow girdle of rough stones and crags,
> A rude and natural causeway, interposed
> Between the water and a winding slope
> Of copse and thicket, leaves the eastern shore
> Of Grasmere safe in its own privacy:
> And there myself and two beloved Friends,
> One calm September morning, ere the mist
> Had altogether yielded to the sun,
> Sauntered on this retired and difficult way.
> – Ill suits the road with one in haste: but we
> Played with our time; and, as we strolled along,
> It was our occupation to observe
> Such objects as the waves had tossed ashore –
> Feather, or leaf, or weed, or withered bough,
> Each on the other heaped, along the line
> Of the dry wreck. And, in our vacant mood,
> Not seldom did we stop to watch some tuft
> Of dandelion seed or thistle's beard,
> That skimmed the surface of the dead calm lake,
> Suddenly halting now – a lifeless stand!
> And starting off again with freak as sudden;
> In all its sportive wanderings, all the while,
> Making report of an invisible breeze
> That was its wings, its chariot, and its horse,
> Its playmate, rather say, its moving soul.
> – And often, trifling with a privilege
> Alike indulged to all, we paused, one now,

And now the other, to point out, perchance
To pluck, some flower or water-weed, too fair
Either to be divided from the place
On which it grew, or to be left alone
To its own beauty. Many such there are,
Fair ferns and flowers, and chiefly that tall fern,
So stately, of the queen Osmunda named;
Plant lovelier, in its own retired abode
On Grasmere's beach, than Naiad by the side
Of Grecian brook, or Lady of the Mere,
Sole-sitting by the shores of old romance.
– So fared we that bright morning: from the fields
Meanwhile, a noise was heard, the busy mirth
Of reapers, men and women, boys and girls.
Delighted much to listen to those sounds,
And feeding thus our fancies, we advanced
Along the indented shore; when suddenly,
Through a thin veil of glittering haze was seen
Before us, on a point of jutting land,
The tall and upright figure of a Man
Attired in peasant's garb, who stood alone,
Angling beside the margin of the lake.
'Improvident and reckless,' we exclaimed,
'The Man must be, who thus can lose a day
Of the mid harvest, when the labourer's hire
Is ample, and some little might be stored
Wherewith to cheer him in the winter time.'
Thus talking of that Peasant, we approached
Close to the spot where with his rod and line
He stood alone; whereat he turned his head
To greet us – and we saw a Man worn down

By sickness, gaunt and lean, with sunken cheeks
And wasted limbs, his legs so long and lean
That for my single self I looked at them,
Forgetful of the body they sustained. –
Too weak to labour in the harvest field,
The Man was using his best skill to gain
A pittance from the dead unfeeling lake
That knew not of his wants. I will not say
What thoughts immediately were ours, nor how
The happy idleness of that sweet morn,
With all its lovely images, was changed
To serious musing and to self-reproach.
Nor did we fail to see within ourselves
What need there is to be reserved in speech,
And temper all our thoughts with charity.
– Therefore, unwilling to forget that day,
My friend, Myself, and She who then received
The same admonishment, have called the place
By a memorial name, uncouth indeed
As e'er by mariner was given to bay
Or foreland, on a new discovered coast;
And POINT RASH-JUDGMENT is the name it bears.

The friends spoken of were Coleridge and my Sister, and
the facts occurred strictly as recorded.

3

'Among the rocks
He went, and still looked up to sun and cloud,
And listened to the wind;'

[*October*] *11th, Saturday*. A fine October morning. Sat in the house working all the morning. William composing. Sally Ashburner learning to mark. After dinner we walked up Greenhead Gill in search of a sheepfold.

We went by Mr Olliff's, and through his woods. It was a delightful day, and the views looked excessively chearful and beautiful, chiefly that from Mr Olliff's field, where our house is to be built. The colours of the mountains soft and rich, with orange fern; the cattle pasturing upon the hill-tops; kites sailing in the sky above our heads; sheep bleating and in lines and chains and patterns scattered over the mountains. They come down and feed on the little green islands in the beds of the torrents, and so may be swept away. The sheepfold is falling away. It is built nearly in the form of a heart unequally divided. Look down the brook, and see the drops rise upwards and sparkle in the air at the little falls, the higher sparkles the tallest. We walked along the turf of the mountain till we came to a cattle track, made by

the cattle which come upon the hills. We drank tea at
Mr Simpson's, returned at about nine – a fine mild night.

October 12th, Sunday. Beautiful day. Sate in the house
writing in the morning while Wm. went into the wood
to compose. Wrote to John in the morning, copied
poems for the L.B.; in the evening wrote to Mrs Rawson.
Mary Jameson and Sally Ashburner dined. We pulled
apples after dinner, a large basket full. We walked before
tea to Bainriggs to observe the many-coloured foliage.
The oaks dark green with yellow leaves, the birches
generally still green, some near the water yellowish, the
sycamore crimson and crimson-tufted, the mountain ash
a deep orange, the common ash lemon-colour, but many
ashes still fresh in their summer green. Those that were
discoloured chiefly near the water. William composing
in the evening. Went to bed at 12 o'clock.

October 13th, Monday. A grey day. Mists on the hills. We
did not walk in the morning. I copied poems on the
Naming of Places. A fair at Ambleside. Walked in the
Black Quarter at night.

[*October*] *14th, Tuesday.* Wm. lay down after dinner – I
read Southey's Spain. The wind rose very high at
evening. Wm. walked out just at bedtime – I went to
bed early. We walked before dinner to Rydale.

[*October 15th,*] *Wednesday.* A very fine clear morning.
After Wm. had composed a little, I persuaded him to go
into the orchard. We walked backwards and forwards.

The prospect most divinely beautiful from the seat; all colours, all melting into each other. I went in to put bread in the oven, and we both walked within view of Rydale. Wm. again composed at the sheepfold after dinner. I walked with him to Wytheburn, and he went on to Keswick. I drank tea, and supped at Mr Simpson's. A very cold frosty air and a spangled sky in returning. Mr and Miss S. came with me. Wytheburn looked very wintry, but yet there was a foxglove blossoming by the roadside.

[*October 18th,*] *Saturday.* A very fine October morning. William worked all the morning at the sheepfold, but in vain. He lay down in the afternoon till 7 o'clock, but could not sleep. I slept, my head better – he unable to work. We did not walk all day.

[*October 19th,*] *Sunday morning.* We rose late, and walked directly after breakfast. The top of G[ras]mere mountains cut off. Rydale was very, very beautiful. The surface of the water quite still, like a dim mirror. The colours of the large island exquisitely beautiful, and the trees still fresh and green were magnified by the mists. The prospects on the west side of the Lake were very beautiful. We sate at the 'two points' looking up to Park's. The lowing of the cattle was echoed by a hollow voice in Knab Scar. We went up Loughrigg Fell and were disappointed with G[ras]mere – It did not look near so beautiful as Rydale. We returned home over the stepping-stones. Wm. got to work. We are not to dine till 4 o'clock. – Dined at ½ past 5 – Mr Simpson dined and drank tea with us. We went to bed immediately after he left us.

[*October*] *20th, Monday*. William worked in the morning at the sheepfold. After dinner we walked to Rydale, crossed the stepping-stones, and while we were walking under the tall oak trees the Lloyds called out to us. They went with us on the western side of Rydale. The lights were very grand upon the woody Rydale hills. Those behind dark and topp'd with clouds. The two lakes were divinely beautiful. Grasmere excessively solemn and the whole lake was calm, and dappled with soft grey ripples. The Lloyds staid with us till 8 o'clock. We then walked to the top of the hill at Rydale. Very mild and warm. About 6 glow-worms shining faintly. We went up as far as the grove. When we came home the fire was out. We ate our supper in the dark, and went to bed immediately. William was disturbed in the night by the rain coming into his room, for it was a very rainy night. The ash leaves lay across the road.

[*October*] *21st, Tuesday*. We walked in the morning past Mr Gell's – a very fine clear sharp sunny morning. We drank tea at the Lloyds. It was very cold in the evening, quite frosty and starlight. Wm. had been unsuccessful in the morning at the sheepfold. The reflection of the ash scattered, and the tree stripped.

[*October 22nd,*] *Wednesday Morning*. We walked to Mr Gell's – a very fine morning. Wm. composed without much success at the sheepfold. Coleridge came in to dinner. He had done nothing. We were very merry. C. and I went to look at the prospect from his seat. In the evening Stoddart came in when we were at tea, and after tea Mr and Miss Simpson with large potatoes and plumbs. Wm. read after supper, *Ruth*, etc.; Coleridge *Christabel*.

[*October*] *23rd, Thursday*. Coleridge and Stoddart went to Keswick. We accompanied them to Wytheburn – a wintry grey morning from the top of the Raise. Grasmere looked like winter, and Wytheburn still more so. We called upon Mrs Simpson and sate 10 minutes in returning. Wm. was not successful in composition in the evening.

[*October*] *24th, Friday*. A very fine morning. We walked before Wm. began to work to the top of the Rydale hills. He was afterwards only partly successful in composition. After dinner we walked round Rydale lake, rich, calm, streaked, very beautiful. We went to the top of Loughrigg. Grasmere sadly inferior. We were much tired – Wm. went to bed till ½ past seven. The ash in the garden green, one close to it bare, the next nearly so.

[*October 25th,*] *Saturday*. A very rainy day. Wm. again unsuccessful. We could not walk, it was so very rainy. We read Rogers, Miss Seward, Cowper, etc.

[*October 26th,*] *Sunday*. Heavy rain all night, a fine morning after 10 o'clock. Wm. composed a good deal in the morning. The Lloyds came to dinner and were caught in a shower. Wm. read some of his poems after dinner.

A terrible night. I went with Mrs Lloyd to Newton's to see for lodgings. Mr Simpson in coming from Ambleside called in for a glass of rum just before we went to bed.

October 27th, Monday. Not a rainy morning. The Hill tops covered with snow. Charles Lloyd came for his wife's glass. I walked home with him past Rydale. When he came I met him as I was carrying some cold meat to Wm. in the Fir-grove, I had before walked with him there for some time. It was a fine shelter from the wind. The coppices now nearly of one brown. An oak tree in a sheltered place near John Fisher's, not having lost any of its leaves, was quite brown and dry. We did not walk after dinner. It was a fine wild moonlight night. Wm. could not compose much, fatigued himself with altering.

[October] 28th, Tuesday. A very rainy night. I was baking bread in the morning and made a giblet pie. We walked out before dinner to our favourite field. The mists sailed along the mountains, and rested upon them, enclosing the whole vale. In the evening the Lloyds came. We drank tea with them at Borwick's and played a rubber at whist – stayed supper. Wm. looked very well – A fine moonlight night when we came home.

[October 31st,] Friday. W. and I did not rise till 1 o'clock. W. very sick and very ill. S. and I drank tea at Lloyds and came home immediately after. A very fine moonlight night – The moon shone like herrings in the water.

*

[*November 4th,*] *Tuesday*. Stoddart left us – I walked a little way with Wm. and him. W. went to the Tarn, afterwards to the top of Seat Sandal. He was obliged to lie down in the tremendous wind. The snow blew from Helvellyn horizontally like smoke – the spray of the unseen water-fall like smoke. Miss Lloyd called upon me – I walked with her past Rydale. Wm. sadly tired – threatenings of the piles.

[*November 5th,*] *Wednesday*. Wm. not well. A very fine clear beautiful winter's day. I walked after dinner to Lloyd's – drank tea and Mrs and Miss Lloyd came to Rydale with me. The moon was rising but the sky was all over cloud. I made tea for William.

November 6th, Thursday. A very rainy morning and night. I was baking bread, dinner and parkins. Charles and P. Lloyd called. Wm. somewhat better. Read *Point Rash Judgment*. The lake calm and very beautiful – a very rainy afternoon and night.

November 7th, Friday. A cold rainy morning. Wm. still unwell. I working and reading *Amelia*. The Michaelmas daisy droops, the pansies are full of flowers, the ashes opposite are green all but one, but they have lost many of their leaves. The copses are quite brown. The poor woman and child from Whitehaven drank tea – nothing warm that day. A very rainy morning. It cleared up in the afternoon. We expected the Lloyds but they did not come. Wm. still unwell. A rainy night.

*

[*November 10th,*] *Monday*. I baked bread. A fine clear frosty morning. We walked after dinner to Rydale village. Jupiter over the hilltops, the only star, like a sun, flashed out at intervals from behind a black cloud.

[*November 11th,*] *Tuesday Morning*. Walked to Rydale before dinner for letters. William had been working at the sheepfold. They were salving sheep. A rainy morning. The Lloyds drank tea with us. Played at cards – Priscilla not well. We walked after they left us to the top of the Rydale hill – then towards Mr Olliff's and towards the village. A mild night, partly cloudy, partly starlight. The cottage lights, the mountains not very distinct.

[*November 12th,*] *Wednesday*. We sate in the house all the day. Mr Simpson called and found us at dinner – a rainy evening – he staid the evening and supper. I lay down after dinner with a headach.

[*November 13th,*] *Thursday*. A stormy night. We sate in the house all the morning. Rainy weather. Old Mr Simpson, Mrs J. and Miss S. drank tea and supped, played at cards, found us at dinner. A poor woman from Hawkshead begged, a widow of Grasmere. A merry African from Longtown.

[*November 14th,*] *Friday*. I had a bad headach. Much wind, but a sweet mild morning. I nailed up trees. Sent Molly Ashburner to excuse us to Lloyds. Two letters from Coleridge, very ill. One from Sara H. One from

S. Lowthian – I wrote to S. Hutchinson and received £3 from her.

[*November 15th,*] *Saturday Morning.* A terrible rain, so William prevented from going to Coleridge's. The afternoon fine and mild – I walked to the top of the hill for a headach. We both set forward at five o'clock after tea. A fine wild but not cold night. I walked with W. over the Raise. It was starlight. I parted with him very sad, unwilling not to go on. The hills, and the stars, and the white waters, with their ever varying yet ceaseless sound, were very impressive. I supped at the Simpsons'. Mr P. walked home with me.

November 16th, Sunday. A very fine warm sunny morning. A letter from Coleridge, and one from Stoddart. Coleridge better. My head aching very much – I sent to excuse myself to Lloyds – then walked to the Cottage beyond Mr Gell's. One beautiful ash tree sheltered, with yellow leaves, one low one quite green. Some low ashes green. A noise of boys in the rocks hunting some animal. Walked a little in the garden when I came home – very pleasant. Now rain came on. Mr Jackson called in the evening when I was at tea, brought me a letter from C. and W. C. better.

[*November 26th,*] *Wednesday.* Well in the morning. Wm. very well. We had a delightful walk up into Easedale. The tops of the mountains covered with snow, frosty and sunny, the roads slippery. A letter from Mary. The Lloyds drank tea. We walked with them near to Ambleside. A beautiful moonlight night. Sara and I walked before [? home]. William very well, and highly poetical.

[*November 27th, Thursday.* Wrote to Tom Hutchinson to desire him to bring Mary with him from Stockton. A thaw, and the ground covered with snow. Sara and I walked before dinner.

[*November 28th,*] *Friday.* Coleridge walked over. Miss Simpson drank tea with us. William walked home with her. Coleridge was very unwell. He went to bed before Wm's return. Great boils upon his neck.

[*December 4th,*] *Thursday.* Coleridge came in just as we finished dinner. Pork from the Simpsons. Sara and I walked round the 2 lakes – a very fine morning. C. ate nothing, to cure his boils. We walked after tea by moonlight to look at Langdale covered with snow, the Pikes not grand, but the Old Man very impressive. Cold and slippery, but exceedingly pleasant. Sat up till half past one.

[*December 5th,*] *Friday Morning.* Terribly cold and rainy. Coleridge and Wm. set forwards towards Keswick, but the wind in Coleridge's eyes made him turn back. Sara and I had a grand bread and cake baking. We were very merry in the evening, but grew sleepy soon, though we did not go to bed till twelve o'clock.

[*December 6th,*] *Saturday.* Wm. accompanied Coleridge to the foot of the Rays. A very pleasant morning. Sara and I accompanied him half-way to Keswick. Thirlmere was very beautiful even more so than in summer. William was not well, had laboured unsuccessfully. Charles Lloyd had called. Sara and I drank tea with Mrs Simpson. A sharp shower met us – it rained a little when we came home – Mr B.S. accompanied us. Miss S. at Ambleside. Wm. tired and not well. A letter from M.H.

[*December 7th,*] *Sunday*. A fine morning. I read. Sara wrote to Hartley, Wm. to Mary, I to Mrs C. We walked just before dinner to the lakeside, and found out a seat in a tree. Windy, but pleasant, Sara and Wm. walked to the waterfalls at Rydale. I was unwell and went to bed till 8 o'clock – a pleasant mild evening – went to bed at 12. Miss Simpson called.

December 8th, Monday. A sweet mild morning. I wrote to Mrs Cookson, and Miss Griffith.

[*December*] *9th, Tuesday*. I dined at Lloyd's. Wm. drank tea. Walked home. A pleasant starlight frosty evening. Reached home at one o'clock. Wm. finished his poem to-day.

Michael

A PASTORAL POEM

If from the public way you turn your steps
Up the tumultuous brook of Greenhead Ghyll,
You will suppose that with an upright path

Your feet must struggle; in such bold ascent
The pastoral mountains front you, face to face.
But, courage! for around the boisterous brook
The mountains have all opened out themselves
And made a hidden valley of their own.
No habitation can be seen; but they
Who journey thither find themselves alone
With a few sheep, with rocks and stones, and kites
That overhead are sailing in the sky.
It is in truth an utter solitude;
Nor should I have made mention of this Dell
But for one object which you might pass by,
Might see and notice not. Beside the brook
Appears a straggling heap of unhewn stones!
And to that simple object appertains
A story – unenriched with strange events,
Yet not unfit, I deem, for the fireside,
Or for the summer shade. It was the first
Of those domestic tales that spake to me
Of shepherds, dwellers in the valleys, men
Whom I already loved; not verily
For their own sakes, but for the fields and hills
Where was their occupation and abode.
And hence this Tale, while I was yet a Boy
Careless of books, yet having felt the power
Of Nature, by the gentle agency
Of natural objects, led me on to feel
For passions that were not my own, and think
(At random and imperfectly indeed)
On man, the heart of man, and human life.
Therefore, although it be a history

Homely and rude, I will relate the same
For the delight of a few natural hearts;
And, with yet fonder feeling, for the sake
Of youthful Poets, who among these hills
Will be my second self when I am gone.

    Upon the forest-side in Grasmere Vale
There dwelt a Shepherd, Michael was his name;
An old man, stout of heart, and strong of limb.
His bodily frame had been from youth to age
Of an unusual strength: his mind was keen,
Intense, and frugal, apt for all affairs,
And in his shepherd's calling he was prompt
And watchful more than ordinary men.
Hence had he learned the meaning of all winds,
Of blasts of every tone; and, oftentimes,
When others heeded not, He heard the South
Make subterraneous music, like the noise
Of bagpipes on distant Highland hills.
The Shepherd, at such warning, of his flock
Bethought him, and he to himself would say,
'The winds are now devising work for me!'
And truly, at all times, the storm, that drives
The traveller to a shelter, summoned him
Up to the mountains: he had been alone
Amid the hearts of many thousand mists,
That came to him, and left him, on the heights.
So lived he till his eightieth year was past.
And grossly that man errs, who should suppose
That the green valleys, and the streams and rocks,
Were things indifferent to the Shepherd's thoughts.

Fields, where with cheerful spirits he had breathed
The common air; hills, which with vigorous step
He had so often climbed; which had impressed
So many incidents upon his mind
Of hardship, skill or courage, joy or fear;
Which, like a book, preserved the memory
Of the dumb animals, whom he had saved,
Had fed or sheltered, linking to such acts
The certainty of honourable gain;
Those fields, those hills – what could they less? had laid
Strong hold on his affections, were to him
A pleasurable feeling of blind love,
The pleasure which there is in life itself.

His days had not been passed in singleness.
His Helpmate was a comely matron, old –
Though younger than himself full twenty years.
She was a woman of a stirring life,
Whose heart was in her house: two wheels she had
Of antique form; this large, for spinning wool;
That small, for flax; and if one wheel had rest
It was because the other was at work.
The Pair had but one inmate in their house,
An only Child, who had been born to them
When Michael, telling o'er his years, began
To deem that he was old – in shepherd's phrase,
With one foot in the grave. This only Son,
With two brave sheep-dogs tried in many a storm,
The one of an inestimable worth,
Made all their household. I may truly say,
That they were as a proverb in the vale

For endless industry. When day was gone,
And from their occupations out of doors
The Son and Father were come home, even then,
Their labour did not cease; unless when all
Turned to the cleanly supper-board, and there,
Each with a mess of pottage and skimmed milk,
Sat round the basket piled with oaten cakes,
And their plain home-made cheese. Yet when the meal
Was ended, Luke (for so the son was named)
And his old Father both betook themselves
To such convenient work as might employ
Their hands by the fireside; perhaps to card
Wool for the Housewife's spindle, or repair
Some injury done to sickle, flail, or scythe,
Or other implement of house or field.

Down from the ceiling, by the chimney's edge,
That in our ancient uncouth country style
With huge and black projection overbrowed
Large space beneath, as duly as the light
Of day grew dim the Housewife hung a lamp;
An aged utensil, which had performed
Service beyond all others of its kind.
Early at evening did it burn – and late,
Surviving comrade of uncounted hours,
Which, going by from year to year, had found,
And left, the couple neither gay perhaps
Nor cheerful, yet with objects and with hopes,
Living a life of eager industry.
And now, when Luke had reached his eighteenth year,
There by the light of this old lamp they sate,

Father and Son, while far into the night
The Housewife plied her own peculiar work,
Making the cottage through the silent hours
Murmur as with the sound of summer flies.
This light was famous in its neighbourhood,
And was a public symbol of the life
That thrifty Pair had lived. For, as it chanced,
Their cottage on a plot of rising ground
Stood single, with large prospects, north and south,
High into Easedale, up the Dunmail-Raise,
And westward to the village near the lake;
And from this constant light, so regular
And so far seen, the House itself, by all
Who dwelt within the limits of the vale,
Both old and young, was named the EVENING STAR.

Thus living on through such a length of years,
The Shepherd, if he loved himself, must needs
Have loved his Helpmate; but to Michael's heart
This son of his old age was yet more dear –
Less from instinctive tenderness, the same
Fond spirit that blindly works in the blood of all –
Than that a child, more than all other gifts
That earth can offer to declining man,
Brings hope with it, and forward-looking thoughts,
And stirrings of inquietude, when they
By tendency of nature needs must fail.
Exceeding was the love he bare to him,
His heart and his heart's joy! For oftentimes
Old Michael, while he was a babe in arms,
Had done him female service, not alone

For pastime and delight, as is the use
Of fathers, but with patient mind enforced
To acts of tenderness; and he had rocked
His cradle, as with a woman's gentle hand.

    And, in a later time, ere yet the Boy
Had put on boy's attire, did Michael love,
Albeit of a stern unbending mind,
To have the Young-one in his sight, when he
Wrought in the field, or on his shepherd's stool
Sate with a fettered sheep before him stretched
Under the large old oak, that near his door
Stood single, and, from matchless depth of shade,
Chosen for the Shearer's covert from the sun,
Thence in our rustic dialect was called
The CLIPPING TREE, a name which yet it bears.
There, while they two were sitting in the shade,
With others round them, earnest all and blithe,
Would Michael exercise his heart with looks
Of fond correction and reproof bestowed
Upon the Child, if he disturbed the sheep
By catching at their legs, or with his shouts
Scared them, while they lay still beneath the shears.
    And when by Heaven's good grace the boy grew up
A healthy Lad, and carried in his cheek
Two steady roses that were five years old;
Then Michael from a winter coppice cut
With his own hand a sapling, which he hooped
With iron, making it throughout in all
Due requisites a perfect shepherd's staff,
And gave it to the Boy; wherewith equipt

He as a watchman oftentimes was placed
At gate or gap, to stem or turn the flock;
And, to his office prematurely called,
There stood the urchin, as you will divine,
Something between a hindrance and a help;
And for this cause not always, I believe,
Receiving from his Father hire of praise;
Though nought was left undone which staff or voice,
Or looks, or threatening gestures, could perform.

But soon as Luke, full ten years old, could stand
Against the mountain blasts; and to the heights,
Not fearing toil, nor length of weary ways,
He with his Father daily went, and they
Were as companions, why should I relate
That objects which the Shepherd loved before
Were dearer now? that from the Boy there came
Feelings and emanations – things which were
Light to the sun and music to the wind;
And that the old Man's heart seemed born again?
Thus in his Father's sight the Boy grew up:
And now, when he had reached his eighteenth year,
He was his comfort and his daily hope.

While in this sort the simple household lived
From day to day, to Michael's ear there came
Distressful tidings. Long before the time
Of which I speak, the Shepherd had been bound
In surety for his brother's son, a man
Of an industrious life, and ample means;
But unforeseen misfortunes suddenly

Had prest upon him; and old Michael now
Was summoned to discharge the forfeiture,
A grievous penalty, but little less
Than half his substance. This unlooked for claim,
At the first hearing, for a moment took
More hope out of his life than he supposed
That any old man ever could have lost.
As soon as he had armed himself with strength
To look his trouble in the face, it seemed
The Shepherd's sole resource to sell at once
A portion of his patrimonial fields.
Such was his first resolve: he thought again,
And his heart failed him. 'Isabel,' said he,
Two evenings after he had heard the news,
'I have been toiling more than seventy years,
And in the open sunshine of God's love
Have we all lived; yet if these fields of ours
Should pass into a stranger's hand, I think
That I could not lie quiet in my grave.
Our lot is a hard lot; the sun himself
Has scarcely been more diligent than I;
And I have lived to be a fool at last
To my own family. An evil man
That was, and made an evil choice, if he
Were false to us; and if he were not false,
There are ten thousand to whom loss like this
Had been no sorrow. I forgive him; – but
'Twere better to be dumb than to talk thus.

'When I began, my purpose was to speak
Of remedies and of a cheerful hope.

Our Luke shall leave us, Isabel; the land
Shall not go from us, and it shall be free;
He shall possess it, free as is the wind
That passes over it. We have, thou know'st,
Another kinsman – he will be our friend
In this distress. He is a prosperous man,
Thriving in trade – and Luke to him shall go,
And with his kinsman's help and his own thrift
He quickly will repair this loss, and then
He may return to us. If here he stay,
What can be done? Where every one is poor,
What can be gained?'
          At this the old Man paused,
And Isabel sat silent, for her mind
Was busy, looking back into past times.
There's Richard Bateman, thought she to herself,
He was a parish-boy – at the church door
They made a gathering for him, shillings, pence
And halfpennies, wherewith the neighbours bought
A basket, which they filled with pedlar's wares;
And, with this basket on his arm, the lad
Went up to London, found a master there,
Who, out of many, chose the trusty boy
To go and overlook his merchandise
Beyond the seas; where he grew wondrous rich,
And left estates and monies to the poor,
And, at his birth-place, built a chapel, floored
With marble which he sent from foreign lands.
These thoughts, and many others of like sort,
Passed quickly through the mind of Isabel,
And her face brightened. The old Man was glad,

And thus resumed: – 'Well, Isabel! this scheme
These two days, has been meat and drink to me.
Far more than we have lost is left us yet.
– We have enough – I wish indeed that I
Were younger; – but this hope is a good hope.
– Make ready Luke's best garments, of the best
Buy for him more, and let us send him forth
To-morrow, or the next day, or to-night;
– If he *could* go, the Boy should go to-night.'

Here Michael ceased, and to the fields went forth
With a light heart. The Housewife for five days
Was restless morn and night, and all day long
Wrought on with her best fingers to prepare
Things needful for the journey of her son.
But Isabel was glad when Sunday came
To stop her in her work: for, when she lay
By Michael's side, she through the last two nights
Heard him, how he was troubled in his sleep:
And when they rose at morning she could see
That all his hopes were gone. That day at noon
She said to Luke, while they two by themselves
Were sitting at the door, 'Thou must not go:
We have no other Child but thee to lose
None to remember – do not go away,
For if thou leave thy Father he will die.'
The Youth made answer with a jocund voice;
And Isabel, when she had told her fears,
Recovered heart. That evening her best fare
Did she bring forth, and all together sat
Like happy people round a Christmas fire.

With daylight Isabel resumed her work;
And all the ensuing week the house appeared
As cheerful as a grove in Spring: at length
The expected letter from their kinsman came,
With kind assurances that he would do
His utmost for the welfare of the Boy;
To which, requests were added, that forthwith
He might be sent to him. Ten times or more
The letter was read over; Isabel
Went forth to show it to the neighbours round;
Nor was there at that time on English land
A prouder heart than Luke's. When Isabel
Had to her house returned, the old Man said,
'He shall depart tomorrow.' To this word
The Housewife answered, talking much of things
Which, if at such short notice he should go,
Would surely be forgotten. But at length
She gave consent, and Michael was at ease.

Near the tumultuous brook of Greenhead Ghyll,
In that deep valley, Michael had designed
To build a Sheepfold; and, before he heard
The tidings of his melancholy loss,
For this same purpose he had gathered up
A heap of stones, which by the streamlet's edge
Lay thrown together, ready for the work.
With Luke that evening thitherward he walked:
And soon as they had reached the place he stopped,
And thus the old Man spake to him: – 'My Son,
To-morrow thou wilt leave me: with full heart
I look upon thee, for thou art the same

That wert a promise to me ere thy birth,
And all thy life hast been my daily joy.
I will relate to thee some little part
Of our two histories; 'twill do thee good
When thou art from me, even if I should touch
On things thou canst not know of. – After thou
First cam'st into the world – as oft befalls
To new-born infants – thou didst sleep away
Two days, and blessings from thy Father's tongue
Then fell upon thee. Day by day passed on,
And still I loved thee with increasing love.
Never to living ear came sweeter sounds
Than when I heard thee by our own fireside
First uttering, without words, a natural tune;
While thou, a feeding babe, didst in thy joy
Sing at thy Mother's breast. Month followed month,
And in the open fields my life was passed
And on the mountains; else I think that thou
Hadst been brought up upon thy Father's knees.
But we were playmates, Luke: among these hills,
As well thou knowest, in us the old and young
Have played together, nor with me didst thou
Lack any pleasure which a boy can know.'
Luke had a manly heart; but at these words
He sobbed aloud. The old Man grasped his hand,
And said, 'Nay, do not take it so – I see
That these are things of which I need not speak.
– Even to the utmost I have been to thee
A kind and a good Father: and herein
I but repay a gift which I myself
Received at others' hands; for, though now old

Beyond the common life of man, I still
Remember them who loved me in my youth.
Both of them sleep together: here they lived,
As all their Forefathers had done; and when
At length their time was come, they were not loth
To give their bodies to the family mould.
I wished that thou should'st live the life they lived:
But, 'tis a long time to look back, my Son,
And see so little gain for three score years.
These fields were burthened when they came to me;
Till I was forty years of age, not more
Than half of my inheritance was mine.
I toiled and toiled; God blessed me in my work,
And till these three weeks past the land was free.
– It looks as if it never could endure
Another Master. Heaven forgive me, Luke,
If I judge ill for thee, but it seems good
That thou should'st go.'

     At this the old Man paused;
Then, pointing to the stones near which they stood,
Thus, after a short silence, he resumed:
'This was a work for us; and now, my Son,
It is a work for me. But, lay one stone –
Here, lay it for me, Luke, with thine own hands.
Nay, Boy, be of good hope; – we both may live
To see a better day. At eighty-four
I still am strong and hale; – do thou thy part;
I will do mine. – I will begin again
With many tasks that were resigned to thee:
Up to the heights, and in among the storms,
Will I without thee go again, and do

All works which I was wont to do alone,
Before I knew thy face. – Heaven bless thee, Boy!
Thy heart these two weeks has been beating fast
With many hopes; it should be so – yes – yes –
I knew that thou could'st never have a wish
To leave me, Luke: thou hast been bound to me
Only by links of love: when thou art gone,
What will be left to us! – But, I forget
My purposes. Lay now the corner-stone,
As I requested; and hereafter, Luke,
When thou art gone away, should evil men
Be thy companions, think of me, my Son,
And of this moment; hither turn thy thoughts,
And God will strengthen thee: amid all fear
And all temptation, Luke, I pray that thou
May'st bear in mind the life thy Fathers lived,
Who, being innocent, did for that cause
Bestir them in good deeds. Now, fare thee well –
When thou return'st, thou in this place wilt see
A work which is not here: a covenant
'Twill be between us; but, whatever fate
Befall thee, I shall love thee to the last,
And bear thy memory with me to the grave.'

The Shepherd ended here; and Luke stooped down,
And, as his Father had requested, laid
The first stone of the Sheepfold. At the sight
The old Man's grief broke from him; to his heart
He pressed his Son, he kissed him and wept;
And to the house together they returned.
– Hushed was that House in peace, or seeming peace,

Ere the night fell: – with morrow's dawn the Boy
Began his journey, and when he had reached
The public way, he put on a bold face;
And all the neighbours, as he passed their doors,
Came forth with wishes and with farewell prayers,
That followed him till he was out of sight.

A good report did from their Kinsman come,
Of Luke and his well-doing: and the Boy
Wrote loving letters, full of wondrous news,
Which, as the Housewife phrased it, were throughout
'The prettiest letters that were ever seen.'
Both parents read them with rejoicing hearts.
So, many months passed on: and once again
The Shepherd went about his daily work
With confident and cheerful thoughts; and now
Sometimes when he could find a leisure hour
He to that valley took his way, and there
Wrought at the Sheepfold. Meantime Luke began
To slacken in his duty; and, at length,
He in the dissolute city gave himself
To evil courses: ignominy and shame
Fell on him, so that he was driven at last
To seek a hiding-place beyond the seas.
There is a comfort in the strength of love;
'Twill make a thing endurable, which else
Would overset the brain, or break the heart:
I have conversed with more than one who well
Remember the old Man, and what he was
Years after he had heard this heavy news.
His bodily frame had been from youth to age

Of an unusual strength. Among the rocks
He went, and still looked up to sun and cloud,
And listened to the wind; and, as before,
Performed all kinds of labour for his sheep,
And for the land, his small inheritance.
And to that hollow dell from time to time
Did he repair, to build the Fold of which
His flock had need. 'Tis not forgotten yet
The pity which was then in every heart
For the old Man – and 'tis believed by all
That many and many a day he thither went,
And never lifted up a single stone.

   There, by the Sheepfold, sometimes was he seen
Sitting alone, or with his faithful Dog,
Then old, beside him, lying at his feet.
The length of full seven years, from time to time,
He at the building of this Sheepfold wrought,
And left the work unfinished when he died.
Three years, or little more, did Isabel
Survive her Husband: at her death the estate
Was sold, and went into a stranger's hand.
The Cottage which was named the EVENING STAR
Is gone – the ploughshare has been through the ground
On which it stood; great changes have been wrought
In all the neighbourhood: – yet the oak is left
That grew beside their door; and the remains
Of the unfinished Sheepfold may be seen
Beside the boisterous brook of Greenhead Ghyll.

THE STORY OF PENGUIN CLASSICS

Before 1946 ...'Classics' are mainly the domain of academics and students, without readable editions for everyone else. This all changes when a little-known classicist, E. V. Rieu, presents Penguin founder Allen Lane with the translation of Homer's Odyssey that he has been working on and reading to his wife Nelly in his spare time.

1946 The Odyssey becomes the first Penguin Classic published, and promptly sells three million copies. Suddenly, classic books are no longer for the privileged few.

1950s Rieu, now series editor, turns to professional writers for the best modern, readable translations, including Dorothy L. Sayers's *Inferno* and Robert Graves's *The Twelve Caesars*, which revives the salacious original.

1960s 1961 sees the arrival of the Penguin Modern Classics, showcasing the best twentieth-century writers from around the world. Rieu retires in 1964, hailing the Penguin Classics list as 'the greatest educative force of the 20th century'.

1970s A new generation of translators arrives to swell the Penguin Classics ranks, and the list grows to encompass more philosophy, religion, science, history and politics.

1980s The Penguin American Library joins the Classics stable, with titles such as *The Last of the Mohicans* safeguarded. Penguin Classics now offers the most comprehensive library of world literature available.

1990s Penguin Popular Classics are launched, offering readers budget editions of the greatest works of literature. Penguin Audiobooks brings the classics to a listening audience for the first time, and in 1999 the launch of the Penguin Classics website takes them online to an ever larger global readership.

The 21st Century Penguin Classics are rejacketed for the first time in nearly twenty years. This world famous series now consists of more than 1,300 titles, making the widest range of the best books ever written available to millions – and constantly redefining the meaning of what makes a 'classic'.

The Odyssey continues ...

The best books ever written

PENGUIN (🐧) CLASSICS

SINCE 1946

Find out more at www.penguinclassics.com